THE COST OF LIBERTY

LIVES OF THE FOUNDERS

EDITED BY JOSIAH BUNTING III

THE COST OF LIBERTY

THE LIFE OF JOHN DICKINSON

William Murchison

ISI
BOOKS

WILMINGTON, DELAWARE

Library of Congress Cataloging-in-Publication Data

Murchison, William P.
  The cost of liberty : the life of John Dickinson / William Murchison.
     pages cm. — (Lives of the founders)
  Includes bibliographical references and index.
  ISBN 978-1-933859-94-1
  1. Dickinson, John, 1732–1808. 2. Statesmen—United States—Biography. 3. United States. Continental Congress—Biography. 4. United States—History—Revolution, 1775–1783. 5. United States—Politics and government—1775–1783. 6. Pennsylvania—History—Revolution, 1775-1783. 7. Delaware—History—Revolution, 1775–1783. I. Title.
  E302.6.D5M87 2013
  973.3092—dc23
  [B]

                              2013026096

ISI Books
Intercollegiate Studies Institute
3901 Centerville Road
Wilmington, DE 19807-1938
www.isibooks.org

Manufactured in the United States of America

For my grandchildren, Brody and Margo,
born into an era of tumult:
that they might hear, and take comfort from,
a tale of fortitude and greatness in the teeth of tumult

CONTENTS

CONTENTS

A NOTE FROM THE PUBLISHER

ISI Books established the Lives of the Founders series to study important figures of the American Founding who have been unjustly forgotten. The United States is certainly indebted to the work and thought of such legendary Founders as Washington, Jefferson, Adams, Madison, Franklin, and Hamilton. But the truth is that hundreds of other men and women made considerable contributions to the Founding.

Moreover, America's course was by no means preordained. When and whether to declare independence from Britain, how to prosecute the Revolutionary War, the precise structure of the new American government—these and many other issues were the subject of serious, and often fierce, debate. By studying lesser-known but influential figures, we get a fuller sense of the contending ideas, controversies, struggles, and particular circumstances that shaped the trajectory of American history.

ISI's Lives of the Founders series reintroduces many of these important thinkers, highlights their contributions, and gets to the bottom of why they have fallen into obscurity. The animating spirit of the series can be seen in the book *America's Forgotten Founders*, which features the results of the first-ever scholarly ranking of neglected Founders and profiles the top ten "forgotten Founders." The other works in the series tell the individual stories of Founders whose names and deeds deserve to be studied and remembered—figures like Luther Martin, the Anti-Federalist polemicist; Gouverneur Morris, who wrote large parts of the Constitution; Nathanael Greene, who after Washington was the most important American general of the War for Independence; Charles Carroll of Carrollton, the only Catholic to sign the Declaration of Independence; and Oliver Ellsworth, a vital force in shaping the Constitution as a Federalist document.

And now ISI is excited to present *The Cost of Liberty*, the first full biography of John Dickinson to appear in a half century. As William Murchison demonstrates in this finely rendered portrait, it is something of a travesty that Dickinson's name is not included among the first rank of American Founders. When Dickinson is remembered, it is usually for something he chose *not* to do—a decision that has earned him a black mark in many quarters. Murchison corrects the record at last, helping us understand what a principled decision it was. More important, he reveals the outsized contributions Dickinson made to the American cause from the 1760s all the way through the late 1780s.

By examining the lives and thought of forgotten Founders like John Dickinson, we can more fully understand the underpinnings of our nation. They allow us to understand the principles and philosophies that guided the Founders, the debates in which they engaged, and how the results of those debates have shaped our country ever since.

THE COST OF LIBERTY

"THE MOST UNDERRATED OF ALL THE FOUNDERS"

MODERNS WHO MAKE THE acquaintance of John Dickinson can be forgiven for finding him, on the whole, both irritable and irritating—hardly the Founding Father likeliest to be singled out, from a room ablaze with talent and inspiration, for some after-hours jollity. He would not be the man to call for punch all around and a lively tune from the fiddler—not with the prospect of a split from the mother country weighing heavily upon his mind and soul.

In HBO's much-honored 2008 series *John Adams*, Mr. Dickinson of Pennsylvania is the specter at America's birthday festivities. While a stick-thumping Adams summons his countrymen to arms and independence, Dickinson, with stricken look and half-shut eyelids, urges caution, demands conciliation, foresees ruin should the mad dash to freedom continue. Replying to such arguments, Adams declares stoutly, "Where he foresees apocalypse, I see hope. I believe, sir, that the hour is come." A toast, sir, to Mr. Adams! As for poor Dickinson, let us make room for him as The Man Who Would Not Sign the Declaration of Independence.

Matters are little different, substantively, in the Broadway musical, and movie, *1776*. A brassier Dickinson faces down Adams with sarcasm and swagger. He hurls at him names and reproaches: "incendiary little man," "madman," and such. The two go at each other with their sticks until separated. The audience knows the direction this tumultuous pathway leads. Once more the course of human events will find the gentleman-ruffian from Pennsylvania standing apart from the jubilation and rejoicing.

Well, not totally apart. Both *John Adams* and *1776* do Dickinson the minimal justice of acknowledging that, having failed to temper his colleagues' enthusiasm for immediate independence, he rode away to serve the colonial cause in uniform—something only one actual Declaration signer, Thomas McKean, did. (He "fought for what he could not vote for," the historian Carl Bridenbaugh has deftly said of Dickinson.)[1]

Still, need we bestow on the gentleman any further thought? Only, perhaps, if we want to understand one of the most complex and influential figures of the entire revolutionary period, someone who was present at all the major assemblages where thinkers and activists charted the young nation's path. At every turn he offered counsel both eloquent and sober. The historian Forrest McDonald has called Dickinson "the most underrated of all the Founders of this nation."[2]

The eclipse of John Dickinson's once-formidable reputation, his reduction to the role of Adams's theatrical foil, is among the ironies and accidents of history. It has to do almost entirely with Dickinson's deeply held doubts regarding the colonies' capacity to achieve independence. The necessity of independence he had come, however slowly, to acknowledge. Was it necessary, all the same, that the task be accomplished according to John Adams's timetable? The perils of precipitate action were large and, equally to the point, largely unexplored. Dickinson, a venerated tribune of the colonists' cause, counseled precaution and delay. Modern reactions are preordained: *How could this man not stand with the great Adams, the great Jefferson, and the other greats at that moment we mark every year with flags and fireworks?* We shall examine the matter in its right sequence.

There is much else to examine in the life of a patriot who wrote with force and intellectual brilliance many of the revolutionary era's major documents—pamphlets, petitions, and speeches, by turns forceful and intricate. He wrote a patriotic song—and probably would have written the Declaration of Independence had he been as hot as Adams to strike off the mother country's shackles at that precise moment. His *Letters from a Farmer in Pennsylvania*, which carefully enunciated the argument for colonial rights, were read and huzzaed throughout the colonies. London took exasperated note of them. They made him the leader, in a rhetorical and sometimes operational sense, of colonial opposition to Britain's transgressions against her overseas sons and daughters. Historians have dubbed Dickinson the "Penman of the Revolution." It is not a bad phrase; nor is it a totally adequate one, suggesting as much as anything else a recording secretary in half-moon spectacles, with head bent low over his journal—a note taker rather than a shaper of mighty events.

Dickinson was, in truth, as much philosopher as writer: a man to whom God had imparted the gifts not merely of expression but also of examination and reflection. Among the large fraternity active in the cause of independence, he gave place, intellectually, to no one. Whenever large decisions were in the offing, John Dickinson's presence and counsel were wanted. In the preconstitutional period he served as chief executive of two different states, Pennsylvania and Delaware. His was the first draft of the Articles of

Confederation. A decade later he was instrumental in arranging the convention that wrote the Constitution—the second grand document to which he never set his name. There was no helping it, the second time. His health had given out. He had to return home before the signing. A friend affixed his name, and there it remains: one more testament to love of country and to character and intellectual wattage. The character he evinced had certain stupendous qualities—akin to those celebrated by the Roman historians from whom he drew wisdom. He was in his own way a bit of a Roman—stubborn as the old consuls and tribunes in defense of principle, willing if it came to that to hand over to the greater good all the blessings he enjoyed, not least immunity from criticism and derision. He was one of the revolutionary era's authentically great men.

He was deeply learned in history and law alike. Out of the deep net of the past, he fished principles that bore directly on current affairs: respect for the admonitions and precedents of past centuries; prudence that called for heeding guideposts and warning signs; the priority of God's determinations in the doings of created humanity; and, with it all, a deep attachment to the God-ordained freedoms that alone enabled forward movement in the human condition—the thing that many call progress. He was no passion-driven pamphleteer, in the manner of Tom Paine, who tossed rhetorical torches onto dry tinder. The Dickinson style was that of the age itself—marked by curves, turnings, and elaborations. Yet he could sum up with clarity and economy when the occasion demanded. Ten words he spoke at the Constitutional Convention in 1787 still cast a glow on the affairs of thinkers and lawmakers. "Experience," Dickinson said, "must be our only guide. Reason may mislead us."[3] Experience was that which we knew, having lived it—the good, the bad, the uplifting, the squalid. By contrast, Reason, and the beauty of the human mind (as shown by

Experience, what else!), could be manipulated into false shapes: made to stand in for speculation, opinion, and surmise. Experience urged mankind to look before leaping, particularly when lives and fortunes—to adopt the language of the Declaration—hung in the balance.

Politics conditions us to seek labels for people in political contexts. Not one but two of our favorite labels generally attach to John Dickinson—"conservative" and "moderate." According to many historians, he was "conservative" insofar as he spoke for the propertied classes and resisted collision with Great Britain, sharing with men of his disposition what the nineteenth-century historian Moses Coit Tyler would call "an uncommon horror of all changes that violated the sequence of established law."[4] He was "moderate" insofar as he stood somewhere between the ardent revolutionism of the Adamses, John and Sam, and the loyalism that, by John Adams's estimate, a third of the colonists shared. Not that his "moderation" was unique among members of the Continental Congress. An entire moderate faction, notes the historian Jack Rakove, believed the British ministry guilty of miscalculation concerning the colonists' grievances. Brought to its senses, the ministry "would abandon a mad policy that could be enforced only at great peril and enormous expense."[5]

A label, though it may expedite discussion, can never say all that needs saying, least of all about a man so complex, even paradoxical, as John Dickinson—a man who early on could argue for measured movement in human affairs yet, in the sunset of life, call blessings down on the revolutionaries of France. A label can disguise subtleties, nuances of thought and action. It should never be stretched the length of a man's, or woman's, form. That can make for bad discourse, bad history—and minimal enlightenment. To box up John Dickinson for consumption as reluctant revolutionary, defender of the fixed and established—any of it—is to serve poorly the cause of telling, and retelling, the tale of how we came to be a people. Not just any people either: one dedicated by all its Founders, whatever their individual motives and interior understandings, to the embrace of life, liberty, and the pursuit of happiness.

Brains, energy, analytical power—one thing more he had. The thing was moral courage of an order not often enough glimpsed today. The shifty, weasel-like Dickinson of the HBO series is hardly a man you picture facing down powerful adversaries whose shouts grow fiercer as their numbers grow greater. Yet so he faced them down—and never, as far as history knows, did he give thought to acting otherwise. Men who had hailed him scurried away from him. He held tight to conviction, hazarding fame and reputation to tell the truth as he saw it to people whose conceptions of truth came more and more to differ from his own. Of his decision to withhold approval of the Declaration of Independence, he would say: "My Conduct this Day, I expect will give the finishing Blow to my once too great and (my integrity considered) now too diminished Popularity."[6] When the end he had hoped to avert came finally to pass, he bravely—possibly gladly—acknowledged the new reality and set forth to serve his country and people by whatever means might become possible. Many such means would become possible during the long and singular life of John Dickinson.

ONE

"THE FIELDS ARE FULL OF PROMISES"

IN THE YOUNG LAND they called home, the Dickinsons bulked larger than most. For one thing they had arrived earlier than most. The great migrations of the seventeenth century had deposited Walter Dickinson on Maryland's Eastern Shore in 1659, shortly after his initial arrival in the Virginia colony. In time the newcomer acquired four hundred acres of tobacco land in Talbot County and another eight hundred in neighboring Delaware's Kent County. The commodious home he built on his Maryland properties he called Crosiadore, in tribute to his lush tobacco fields. The name, from the French *Croix d'Or*, meant Cross of Gold.

As wealth and distinction increased, so the family grew, one generation succeeding another. To Walter's grandson Samuel and his second wife, Mary Cadwalader, a well-educated member of a solid Philadelphia Quaker family, was born, on November 13, 1732, a son, named John for his mother's father. A second son, Thomas, followed in 1734, only to die as a child. A third son, Philemon, born in 1739, became a revolutionary war general of some note.[1]

The neighborhood of Crosiadore, for all the bounty of its soil, presented real drawbacks. It was arduously distant from Philadelphia, the uncontested center of life in the "middle" colonies of Pennsylvania, New Jersey, and Delaware. (The last was a mostly self-governing appendage of Pennsylvania.) Then there was the obstructive behavior of the local Quakers, in whose fold the Dickinsons lived out their religious life. In 1739 Samuel's only daughter, Betsy—one of just two living children out of the nine born to him and his first wife, Judith—wished to wed a highly respectable non-Quaker, the son of Maryland's chief justice. The Quakers would have none of it. The Third Haven Quarterly Meeting pronounced the union "disorderly" for occurring outside the Meeting. Samuel, for his part, was determined that Betsy should marry the man of her choice. No rebuke fell upon him, but he swiftly disassociated himself from the Meeting.

The disadvantages of the neighborhood became more and more obvious. Samuel resolved to relocate his seat of activity nearer the six square miles of rich wheat land he had acquired in Kent County, Delaware, with its ready access to Philadelphia by means of the Delaware River—or, alternatively, two days by horseback or carriage. He turned over Crosiadore and its lands to Betsy and her brother Henry and gave orders for the construction of a suitably imposing Georgian-style house at Jones Neck, some five miles below the new village of Dover—Delaware's future capital. Here he brought his family in January 1740. Here, in spirit at least, John Dickinson dwelt for the rest of his long, active life, never ceasing to love the house and its lands, returning to them whenever he could. "All nature is blooming around me," he would write during one such rural reunion in the late 1780s, "and the fields are full of promises."[2]

The young John Dickinson received the somewhat loose-jointed but appropriately dignified upbringing experienced by the children of the colonies' rural gentry. There were rides and romps, and also lessons. He took to the latter with special keenness. Samuel Dickinson engaged for his older son an Irish-born tutor so able he would work his way up eventually to the chancellorship of Delaware. William Killen was only ten years older than John. By Isaac Sharpless's account, Killen filled his charge's mind "with high ideals and aided him to secure an English style remarkably simple and elegant and effective, which no one of that day, except perhaps Franklin, equalled."[3] If credit properly belongs to Killen, he merits more than a cold paragraph in the chronicle of the times. His pupil's prose, in the 1760s and '70s, became a slingshot, carrying throughout the colonies and England itself the deepest, choicest arguments for the justice of the colonial cause.

It became clear enough to all concerned that, much as John might love the land, he was better cut out to be a lawyer than a farmer. As a cousin would later say of him, "His proficiency in his studies filled the minds of his parents with delight."[4] Samuel Dickinson was himself a lawyer, with high respect for books and learning. It was resolved that John would go, in 1750, to Philadelphia to read law under one of the city's legal luminaries, John Moland. A fellow Moland student was George Read, who became Dickinson's warm and longtime friend, and eventually chief justice of Delaware.

The legal profession in those days was less a profession, by subsequent standards, than an association of independently, not to say irregularly, trained men with a common outlook concerning duties, responsibilities, and hope of gain. "During the whole colonial period," writes Daniel Boorstin, "America probably did not produce a single lawyer who was deeply learned by the strict English standards. Americans tended to be smatterers and admirers of the law, never its high priests."[5] Frequently the colonial litigant found a layman sitting as judge in his cause, applying common sense to a given situation, insofar as the various parties might agree with another's ad hoc definition of common sense. In a country without law schools, books of law were not easily procured. (Sir William Blackstone's formative and formidable *Commentaries on the Laws of England* would not be published until 1765–1769.)

Colonial law practice did, however, produce a few grave and worthy eminences. There was Moland, for instance; throughout the colonies were others. The Dickinsons decided John would join their company. It would be advisable in that event for him to cross the Atlantic and take up the study of English law at the source. Thus, in 1753, he took ship for London, to join the Middle Temple.

TO LONDON: "PUTTING IN MY LITTLE OAR"

The privilege of study at the Middle Temple was not unique for young colonials. It was considerable all the same: an extended sojourn at the source of English guarantees of hallowed rights. John Dickinson's time at the Middle Temple influenced decisively not just his appraisals of method under law but also his understanding of the manner in which inclinations become claims, claims become rights, and rights take on a solemnity and power capable of binding a people together.

In no country besides Britain were the rights of subjects and the duties of rulers spelled out so specifically and candidly—the consequence of power collisions dating from Magna Carta, in 1215, that had produced agreements designed to avert future collisions. The majesty of law oversaw and ruled for or against—in theory, at all events—the passions of those who came to its notice.

English history had prepared Englishmen to think of themselves as shielded from arbitrary or purely spontaneous actions on their rulers' part. This was by slow and grave process of accretion. The common law—"that ancient collection of unwritten maxims and customs . . . excellently adapted to the genius of the English nation," Blackstone called it—was no abstraction.[6] It was an organism, with breath of its own, nurtured by practice and precedent. It proved an important bulwark against tyranny of the *roi soleil* variety, at the court of Louis XIV and elsewhere on the continent. The great Lord Coke, who would become England's first lord chief justice, chose rashly (as it turned out) to throw at King James I the majestic prescription of the thirteenth-century jurist Bracton: *Rex non debet esse sub homine sed sub Deo et lege*—the king ought not be under man but under God and the law. At which claim against the undue assertion of his royal powers, James "fell into the highest indignation as the like was never knowne in him." Coke, in understandable alarm, "fell flatt on all fower."[7] In due course he rose. Before his death in 1634, when James's son Charles I reigned, he had entrenched all the more deeply in his countrymen's minds the doctrine of law as larger than the lot of them. As free countries went in the eighteenth century, none was so free as Britain, or so proud of its freedoms. Blackstone explained it: "The absolute rights of every Englishman (which, taken in a political and extensive sense, are usually called their liberties), as they are founded on nature and reason, so they are coeval with our form of government."

A lawyer was a principal custodian of this great tradition: no mere mechanic of words and phrases, meaningless in themselves. His touch, rightly applied, brought life to ideas and truths with bearing on the daily condition of men and women. Not that the lawyer's training quite matched the importance of the vocation.

Through the four Inns of Court—the Inner and Middle Temples, Gray's Inn, and Lincoln's Inn, named for the hostels where students once lived—ran the exclusive path to membership in the English bar. The call to the bar was in fact a call to the bar of the Inn itself. The problem, from the eighteenth-century law student's standpoint, was that the Inns had not flourished as educational institutions for something like two centuries. With the passage of time, their pedagogical methods became more and more haphazard and uncoordinated. One scholar calls legal education, in John Dickinson's day, "a very melancholy topic."[8]

There was, to begin with, no effective teaching at the Inns. The student of law was "left to his own resources"—"obliged to get his knowledge of law by means of undirected reading and discussion, and by attending in chambers, in a law office, or in the courts."[9] The courts themselves were not always prepossessing institutions. "Counsel were distinguishable from the idlers waiting to hear the judgments, or the shoppers chatting, only by their gown and bands," notes Liza Picard in her examination of life in mid-eighteenth century London. "Far from there being silence in court, Counsel had to contend with spectators 'in deep discourses upon some irrelevant subject . . . and young ladies actually sewing each other's clothes together amidst titters and suppressed laughter.'" Blackstone, a Middle Templar, lamented the manner in which "a raw and inexperienced youth" was expected "to sequester himself from the world, and by a tedious lonely process to extract the theory of law from a mass of undigested learning; or else by an assiduous attendance on the courts to pick up theory and practice together, sufficient to qualify him for the ordinary run of business."[10] Mother England's concept of adequacy in legal education doubtless exceeded that of her colonial brood, but perhaps not by so very much.

The laxity of the Inns, as John Dickinson encountered it, cannot have been precisely what he had contemplated as he shuffled through legal papers and law books at John Moland's law office in Philadelphia. For all that, Middle Temple training was, in the colonies, prestigious and desirable. If the North American colonies partook of the mother country's legal and constitutional heritage, why not sup at her table, at least for a time? The colonists, accordingly, had been comparatively heavy patrons of the Inns since the late seventeenth century. "This vogue of the Inns," says Boorstin, "seems to have increased unaccountably after about 1750: of approximately 236 American-born members of the Inns of Court before 1815, over half were admitted between 1750 and 1775."[11] South Carolina supplied about a third of the total, Virginia a fourth. Maryland sent more to the Inns than Pennsylvania, New York, or Massachusetts. Five signers of the Declaration of Independence—including all four South Carolinians present—had studied at the Middle Temple. The fifth, Dickinson's friend Thomas McKean of Pennsylvania, had begun his labors there just two years after Dickinson's return, in 1756. Fifteen-year-old John Rutledge of South Carolina—elder brother of the Declaration signer Edward—took up residence at the Middle Temple less than a year after Dickinson's arrival. Already ensconced there was William Drayton of South Carolina. Some of Dickinson's English contemporaries at the Middle Temple would achieve distinction: among them, Edward Thurlow, the future lord chancellor who was a noted foe of colonial reconciliation save on the Crown's terms, and William Cowper, the poet, translator of Homer, and author of well-known evangelical hymns. Blackstone had joined in 1741, receiving his call to the bar in 1746.

Young John Dickinson reached England on December 10, 1753, after a fifty-nine-day voyage, the greater portion of which, so he informed his parents, he spent "confined . . . to the cabbin and mostly to my bed" by illness.[12] Then, London itself. The foremost city of the British Empire, its origins dating to the Romans' Londinium, was a cauldron of wonders and contradictions: refinement and elegance; squalor and crime; Hogarthian horrors and classical town houses; church steeples soaring above warehouses and wharves that received and distributed the goods of the world; a wide and murky river leading wistfully in one direction to the pastures of Oxfordshire, in the other direction to the gray terrors of the ocean. "When a man is tired of London, he is tired of life, for there is in London all that life can afford," the eminent, and quintessential, Londoner Dr. Samuel Johnson observed.[13] Johnson's monumental *Dictionary* would come forth, to vast acclaim, during Dickinson's time in the city. Although the French might claim Paris as the center of civilized endeavor, there were impressive countervailing arguments for London, whose 650,000 residents (give or take 50,000) not only outnumbered the Parisians by 20 percent or so but also constituted more than 10 percent of all the people in England. Yet it was a place compact enough that a pair of gentlemen who set out to walk around it in 1763 found the task took a mere seven hours.[14]

No twenty-two-year-old from colonial Philadelphia could have seen anything like it, inasmuch as there was nothing anywhere like it to see. Dickinson—in exceedingly mature and sophisticated letters to his parents—conveyed just the sense of place and occasion that they must have hoped for as they parted with their son. "More is learned of mankind here in a month," he wrote, "than can be in a year in any other part of the world." Again: "London is the place where a person may learn Truth, where, unless he is an absolute fool, he may see human nature in all shapes." He turned with eagerness to his new manner of life. From the shared chambers he occupied at first, with new floors and a laundress to light the fire at 7 a.m. and put on the kettle, he moved in the spring to chambers of his own. His habit was to rise at 5 a.m. and read for eight hours, "which is as much as I can or ought to do . . . I dine at four, & am in bed by ten."[15]

There was, of course, a great deal to do. The likes of Coke and Sir Edmund Plowden, the Tudor scholar and jurist, kept company in Dickinson's chambers with the noble Romans in Tacitus, Cicero, and Sallust. Dickinson was piecing together, bit by bit, a comprehensive view of the affairs of mankind and the law's role as arbiter. "Amongst others," he wrote in August 1754, "I am putting in my little oar, & exerting my small strength . . . convinced . . . that there cannot be upon earth a nobler employment than the defence of innocence, the support of justice, & the preservation of peace and harmony amongst men. These are the offices of my profession, & if my abilities are but equal to my inclination, they will not be undischa[r]gd by me." The intellectual aspects of law practice suited him as well: "I may say, without boasting, I have taken as much pleasure in unraveling an intricate point of law as a florist receives when he sees some favorite flower, which he has long tended himself, at last unfold its glowing colours & breathe its sweet perfumes." "The barr" itself he found "a perfect comment upon the written law, & every great man at it is in some measure a master & instructor to the young students who have the wisdom to attend here."[16]

He paid due attention to the city's sights—always with a philosophical eye. The "walks frequented by the antient sages of the law" kindled veneration in him. Among the city's monuments he deduced that life "teaches how trivial is every thing in it." Westminster Abbey, where he liked to walk "with pleasing awe," showed him "the ravages made by TIME in the honours of kings & the most illustrious families." On visiting a small parish church, he was struck to find Sir Francis Bacon lying "amongst ploughmen and labourers." Here, clearly, was a young man who took the long view of things: passionate enough, but able to focus passion on large objects. Among certain things he was coming to know about himself was the complexity of his own instincts. In his heart, the law and the land vied for attention. A journey to Kent—England's garden—reinforced his love of nature and the furrowed earth. He found—unaccountably, given the reasons he had come to England in the first place—"a great attraction" toward "the noble retirement of Kent." He might, he told his father, become a useful community member there, "by prosecuting debts for Sunday cloaths." Or he might, after acquiring some honors, "turn husbandman & till the bed which in a short time will receive me. But before I go that far, I must take care that my first steps be well planted."[17]

This was no doubt to say that his prior, and great, vocation awaited him. On February 8, 1757, the Middle Temple called John Dickinson to the bar. It was time at last to go home. He had a foot planted now on each side of the ocean. What most of his countrymen saw dimly, if at all, as they looked eastward to England, he had more than seen: he had walked its twisted streets, smelled its robust smells.

He had even met the king. In London, Dickinson called on Thomas Penn, a son of Pennsylvania's founder and proprietor, the great Quaker William Penn. Thomas had returned to his native England and become an Anglican after managing the proprietorship for a few years. Penn undertook to present his new acquaintance, the son of a distinguished colonial family, at the court of George II, who had by then reigned for three decades (along the way, as legend would have it, instituting the custom of rising for Handel's "Hallelujah" chorus). The meeting persuaded Dick-

inson that he had met "the greatest & best king upon earth."[18]
There would be no such meetings with the third George, though
that sovereign would come to know John Dickinson's name well
indeed.

THE WAYS OF THE LAW

That five Middle Templars were, unlike John Dickinson, glad
enough to sign the Declaration of Independence was in part a
function of chronology. All four South Carolinians were at least a
decade younger than he; only Thomas McKean, his fellow Pennsylvanian and law student, was of his generation. The ways of English law, and of the Inns, had had more time to sink into Dickinson's consciousness. The ways of the law were large and grave; they
had not blossomed overnight, nor had their fruit grown randomly.
Careful hands had guided their formation: pruning, watering, and
shaping, as circumstances required. The old laws might in time
cease to serve as intended originally. Was not the law's age, even so,
a reminder of the need for prudence of the sort any good surgeon
might apply to the relief of an injury? Did—a further, if unan-
swerable, point—Dickinson's instinctive love of fields and forests
fuse in his mind with the instinct to love the law as one more vital
organism to protect from axes and cross saws?

Long after the young lawyer's return to America, the impress
of the Middle Temple remained to be recognized. Not on John
Dickinson's brow: behind it, rather.

TWO

"AN IMMENSE BUSTLE IN THE WORLD"

THE CLUTTER OF SHIPS' masts and the roofs of trim brick build-
ings could be seen from some distance as sailing craft slowly made
their way up the broad Delaware River. To portside lay the fairest
city in America, and the busiest: its docks aswarm with comings
and goings, starts and completions, of every kind and size. The
Quakers who built Philadelphia, street by street, square by square,
testified powerfully to their talent for cohesion and industry. The
port city to which John Dickinson returned in 1757 was no North
American London; it was, nevertheless, without equal among the
North American continent's upstart towns and villages. Its central
location—athwart the lines of communication between Charleston and Williamsburg to the south and Boston and New York
to the north—afforded the city exceptional leverage in colonial
affairs. Here the great councils of the colonies would gather to
discuss and seek remedies for a discontent that ripened to exaspera-
tion, then anger, over British rules and regulations. Philadelphia
would become in short order the fulcrum of American nationhood,

irrespective of whether all its people sought identical ends through identical means.

With an estimated thirty thousand inhabitants by 1776, Philadelphia was the continent's most populous city—indeed, its only real city, compared to which, says David Hawke in his history of Pennsylvania in the lead-up to independence, "all other so-called cities in American were only overgrown villages." "The bulk" of its people, Hawke continues, "lived as comfortably as any people on earth in the eighteenth century"[1]—which would suggest that various Londoners had cause to look with envy on their attractions and amenities.

The Swedes, knowing a good site when they saw one, had settled there in 1638, along the Delaware River. By 1682 the Quakers were in charge. Of all improbable subduers of wilderness, the Quakers were possibly the unlikeliest: each one beset and driven by the call to discover for himself, according to Inner Light, the path to righteousness. The new colony of Pennsylvania ("Penn's Woods"), which King Charles II entrusted to William Penn in satisfaction of a debt owed Penn's father, became the center of Quaker witness and endeavor. The Quakers were much more, and far more interesting, than the oddly dressed folk on modern-day cereal boxes; they possessed brains and enterprise, so that Pennsylvania, under their aegis, grew and thrived, a symbol of what was possible in the new world, given time and hard work. They were perhaps ideal settlers—thrifty, ambitious, tolerant, peaceable. And devoted to their religious point of view, however off-center that view— owing to doctrinal pacifism and egalitarianism—might appear to outsiders. (The irregularities of Quaker worship were likewise conspicuous: rows and rows of silent participants waiting for the spirit to give one, or many, of them utterance.) Neither the Puritans of Massachusetts nor the Anglicans of Virginia made their respective colonies work so well for them as did the Quakers of Pennsylvania. "There was perfect liberty," writes the nineteenth-century English historian W. E. H. Lecky, "and the prevailing spirit was gentle, humane, pacific, and keenly money-making."[2] Small wonder that Pennsylvania could be seen as beckoning to the whole world. In poured Anglican, Scots-Irish Presbyterian, and German Lutheran settlers. By 1770 they had reduced the Quakers to a mere seventh of the Pennsylvania's overall population without diminishing the colony's prominence and prosperity.[3]

In Philadelphia, "City of Brotherly Love" and capital of the colony, the appurtenances of civilization were everywhere to be seen, tasted, and enjoyed. Buttonwood and willow trees lined the right-angled main streets. Pedestrians who trod the brick or flagstone sidewalks could rely generally on posts that kept the jurisdiction free of carriages. Merchants with an eye for custom often fitted out the area in front of their shops with cobblestones or paving blocks—an early instance of private-sector initiative to satisfy public needs. Whale-oil lamps suspended from posts illuminated most principal streets from 1751 forward—by which time a Philadelphia deputy postmaster, Benjamin Franklin, was already immersed in figuring out the properties and possibilities of electricity. Within a year, his kite experiment would demonstrate that lightning and electricity were the same. To Franklin, Philadelphians owed a more immediate civic boon—the commencement of mail service three times a week between their city and New York. Service to Virginia and Baltimore and beyond began by 1767, in time to spread new political sentiments about taxation and colonial rights.

Philadelphia's wealth had fostered not only an aristocratic fox-hunting club with its own uniforms but also shops for the production of chairs, tables, sofas, and tall-case clocks, whose elegance and marks of craftsmanship commend them still to collectors and other aesthetes. Each year from 1749 to 1752 an average of 403 ships cleared port from the city. On a single day in 1754, a Swedish missionary counted 117 large ships at anchor in the Delaware River. Vessels outbound from Philadelphia carried wheat, corn, flour, bread, bacon, beef, barrel staves and headings, lumber, pig iron, flaxseed, furs, and deerskins. From England and the West Indies came sugar, molasses, spices, tools, machinery, kitchen utensils, books, and like necessities of the good life.

Philadelphia, at midcentury, had a library, a fire department, a police force, newspapers, a hospital, and a college. The colonial history scholar Louis B. Wright judged that, for sheer intellectual vitality, no other colonial city was Philadelphia's match—an observation with which Philadelphians of the era would have happily concurred. A "poetical description" of the city, from 1730 (less than half a century after the Quakers' coming), held with just a touch of vainglory that "Europe shall mourn her ancient fame declined / And Philadelphia be the Athens of Mankind." As they became rich, the very Quakers who saw themselves— theoretically—as simple folk increasingly went in for show and display. "Such men," says the sociologist E. Digby Baltzell, "simply assumed their superior worth." As did, of course, those wealthy non-Quakers whose numbers were multiplying. A wilderness paradise founded on renunciation, as idealists from Massachusetts southward quickly learned to their discomfort, was hard to protect from the rough realities of life in a rich new land.[4]

As seat of government for the proprietorship, Philadelphia had not only the gear of commerce but also a State House of special grandeur, where in the course of time grand events would take place. A contemporary reported that the building was "adorned on ye outside with rustic corners and marble panels, between the two stories." Here the state's Assembly and Supreme Court met. There was a tower with bell: located, however, in a wooden part of the steeple that was "in such a ruinous condition that they are afraid to ring the bell, lest by so doing the steeple should fall down." When, in the summer of 1776, there arose a cause for rejoicing, Philadelphians would find means to surmount that difficulty.[5] In the 1750s, few if any envisioned a time when the Mosaic exhortation inscribed on the bell—"Proclaim liberty throughout all the land unto all the inhabitants thereof" (Leviticus 25:10)—would apply to their local situation. The political temperature of the town was placid, deferential. Prior to 1775, as the patriot statesman Joseph Reed would recall a decade later, "no King ever had more loyal subjects; or any country more affectionate colonists" than the people of Philadelphia, Pennsylvania.[6]

THE FIRST TEST

When John Dickinson returned to his adopted city to commence law practice, the prospects for a Middle Templar endowed with wealth, breeding, and good family were notable. Intellect alone might have commended him to a large and influential clientele. Fortunately, it may be, the eighteenth century lacked the aptitude of successor centuries for artificial measurements of intelligence. We thus have no IQ rankings or test scores by which to rate Dickinson alongside his contemporaries. From his writings and speeches over the years, nonetheless, there emerges a pattern: scholarly knowledge of history and philosophy, the proof of wide reading; a clarity of writing style evidencing clarity of thought and analysis; a facility at the use of historical parallels to illuminate present-day events; withal, a dignity of approach to the most heated questions (not excluding occasional ventures into contempt and sarcasm—our man had a temper, fueled by sensitivity to perceived insult). The intellectual equipment of John Dickinson, on sheer external evidence, was hard to equal, far less surpass, at the middle of the century and afterward. Even among the "demigods" of his time, to give the Founding Fathers the name they sometimes still bear, his gifts were of a superior cast. He could hold his own in any company, including that of the Founder generally represented as his staunchest adversary, John Adams.

Dickinson was no original thinker, nor did he desire to become such. He scoured about, in the best common-law manner, for precedents on which to found his reasonings. The wisdom of the past was his subject matter and inspiration. What the wise and the just had found good and useful—not to mention true—he saw as invaluable matter for examination. The light of the past was just that—light. It shone on the pathway ahead, as on the path behind. Better, by and large, to know the way than to guess at it, was John Dickinson's stubbornly held notion.

If the head on his shoulders was impressive, the frame that supported it was a different matter. Tall, and thin as a fence railing, Dickinson possessed an arrestingly long nose but also, a good deal of the time, the appearance of illness and fatigue. Uncertain health would dog him all his days. The eighteenth century might have been more generally healthy than previous epochs, but that is not saying so very much. Fevers, agues, gout, malaria, smallpox, and assorted aches and pains stalked the population, picking off the weaker or less happily situated. Dickinson would live to the ripe age of seventy-six, but at times his survival seemed a near-run thing. His illnesses and complaints could lay him low for months at a time, as in England, where during his first summer he suffered from "a most violent fit of fever & ague." "An uneasiness" in his chest kept him out of London from June until October.[7] John Adams, on meeting him for the first time in 1774, at the onset of the First Continental Congress, when Dickinson was forty-one, pronounced him "a Shadow—tall, but slender as a Reed—pale as ashes. One would think at first sight that he could not live a Month." That was not the whole of it, to be sure. "Upon a more attentive Inspection," Adams continued, "he looks as if the Springs of Life were strong enough to last many Years." Indeed they proved so.[8] Friend and foe alike would discover there was within John Dickinson a mental toughness of larger advantage to him, no doubt, than everyday heartiness. Any who supposed he might with repetitive or emotional arguments wear Dickinson down had put money on the wrong horse.

The Dickinson who returned to Philadelphia brought with him a sense of occasion and personal destiny. He had already a sense of his capacity to do things—to make a difference in the life unfolding before him. A few months after arriving in London, he had written to his father: "When I see men advanced by their own application to the highest honours of their country, my breast beats for fame! . . . I quicken at their glory."[9] Back home, he fit snugly enough into Philadelphia's ambitious and resourceful Quaker culture, in spite of own tenuous ties to Quakerism.

The question of Quakerism's relationship to Dickinson's political thinking will arise soon enough in the course of this narrative. Did the Friends have other effects on him? We have noticed earlier Samuel Dickinson's willingness to see a daughter married outside the Quaker Meeting—and the paternal outrage that flared when the Meeting declared the marriage unacceptable. The episode can only have left a bad taste in the mouths of the family regarding Quakerism. Dickinson, as Isaac Sharpless sums it up in his study of the faith, was "not much of a Quaker." "His association with Friends was probably, at least in early life, not much more than nominal," though "in his later life he was closely associated with Friends, and was probably a member."[10] He was not, then, in the fully rounded sense, a Quaker; neither was he *not* one. "He undoubtedly," says Sharpless, "represented and dignified the Quaker idea of the presence of liberty"—in a way, perhaps, that made his powers all the more formidable as he defended liberty. In any case, Dickinson plied a professional and social path that criss-crossed denominational lines. Firm and well-schooled Christian as he was, he was anything but sectarian. He would write later of the impossibility, as he found it, of belonging to any organized expression of the Christian faith. All churches had their points; all had their deficiencies. He could not choose, nor would he.[11]

The man of the law becomes a public figure by virtue of his professional calling. Into the maw of general affairs he can find himself sucked without warning—for that matter, without resistance. So it happened with young John Dickinson. He quickly found law practice agreeable both to his tastes and to his prospects in life. By 1763 he was able to inform his mother, "Money flows in, and my vanity has been very agreeably flattered of late."[12] A fellow Philadelphian, Benjamin Kite, would years later recollect Dickinson's skills in the courtroom: "J. Galloway and J. Dickinson were my favorite pleaders; the first, perhaps, because he was the head of the party to which my friends belong,—but the other was really a beautiful speaker."[13] Not that he was all usufructs and *quo warrantos*. Another fellow townsman saw, perhaps, to the heart of Dickinson's intellectual constitution. His legal knowledge, while "respectable" in the eye of this onlooker, was not preeminent: "his attention was directed to historical and political studies."[14] To put the matter another way, Dickinson was more architect than drafts-man, with more of his care and focus brought to bear on vault and clerestory than on masonry. There would be intimations of this trait in his political writings.

Not the least of his achievements, from the wider historical perspective, was to take into his office as apprentice a young Scottish immigrant and graduate of the University of St. Andrews, James Wilson. Wilson was himself destined to become a Founding Father: a signer both of the Declaration and of the Constitution.[15] His temperament proved more volatile than his preceptor's when it came to British infractions of colonial rights; still, the two men's friendship endured.

Dickinson's entry into electoral politics had been practically predetermined. He was ambitious; he cared for public affairs; he brought to their consideration a mind of the first rate, steadied by observation and deep reading. Moreover, he lived at a moment whose political necessities increasingly cried out for just those attributes. The year of his father's death, 1760, marked his accession to politics. That October he won election to the Assembly of the "lower counties," which was to say, the three Delaware counties that prior to the Revolution belonged to Pennsylvania yet maintained their own legislative body. The precocious and well-connected Dickinson became that assembly's speaker before moving upstairs as it were, winning a 1762 special election to fill a vacancy in the Pennsylvania Assembly. To his friend George Read he wrote with beguiling candor: "I confess that I should like to make an immense bustle in the world, if it could be done by virtuous actions."[16] He soon enough had his chance. This occurred when the polymathic Benjamin Franklin—as much politician as scientist—proposed a change in the colony's manner of government. Franklin, with the backing of the so-called Quaker party that controlled the Assembly, sought to place Pennsylvania under the direct rule of the English king, who by this time was George III.

In view of events soon to ensue in English-colonial relations, an obvious question arises: What could Franklin have been thinking about? A deep game of local politics lay at the bottom of the matter. Pennsylvania had outgrown the Penns, who retained executive power over the colony and its 183,000 residents even as the province's radically democratic Charter of Privileges (1701) provided for both a democratically elected Assembly and liberty of religious conscience. Upon the death of the spaciously minded William Penn in 1718, the proprietorship had devolved upon his widow, Hannah, as executrix for their four sons: John, Thomas, Richard, and Dennis. Thereafter, the semifeudal characteristics of the people-proprietor relationship began to irritate, then vex. In all, the Penns owned 35,361,300 acres, which, according to Dickinson's nineteenth-century biographer, Charles J. Stillé, they "managed like a large farm, with little regard after the death of the founder of this Province, for the welfare and interests of those who had been induced by him to settle here." Under William Penn's grant from Charles II, the original proprietor and his heirs were "true and Absolute Proprietaries," from whom the Crown exacted only a nominal yearly rent. The Penns—kings of a sort—could grant or lease lands, incorporate cities, and set up manors, towns, and counties. They could make laws to which the "advice, assent, and approbation" of the province's freemen, or their deputies, was required. Says the historian Winfred Root: "The proprietor was both the absolute lord of the soil and the source of all political power."[17]

It was not the government designed by a kindly Nature for a loosely buttoned set of colonists on an unruly frontier, where there was alarm about the Indians and constant feuding over the Assembly's wish to tax the proprietor's estates to raise revenue. In late 1763 Presbyterian westerners of mostly Scotch-Irish extraction (a combative race by nature) augmented the tensions by slaughtering some peaceful Indians. They threatened to enter Philadelphia itself, terrifying the Quakers and Anglicans. Nothing in these circumstances quite conduced to the general welfare. Adjustments seemed not merely inevitable but also essential.

Mere adjustment was, nevertheless, the last thing on Franklin's mind. He sought something like revolution, if in the very odd form of handing over major authority to a hereditary monarch situated abroad. The Assembly, wishing to tax the Penns' estates, had sent Franklin to London in 1757 (the year of Dickinson's return to America) to see how the cause might be advanced. Franklin's five years there as colonial representative had persuaded him that the Turkey carpet, and all tea tables resting upon it, had to be pulled from beneath the proprietors' feet. Accordingly, as H. W. Brands, a modern biographer of Franklin, puts it, "in the ebullience of his Britishness, he embraced royal rule as the solution to the problems of the province." He may likewise have wished that a grateful Crown might bestow on him a sizable grant of land once the handover of power was accomplished. The colony's respected agent in England, Richard Jackson, had assured Franklin as early as 1758 that the Crown could be counted on to protect the rights that Pennsylvanians enjoyed under their charter. Jackson later modified that viewpoint, but Franklin by then had the bit between his teeth. The father of electricity, and of intercity mail service, was no force at which to yawn. He moved with energy and dispatch to perfect his plans. A report in March 1764 by an Assembly committee on which he sat gave tongue to the grievances that many felt against the proprietors. Franklin published the following month a pamphlet furthering his arguments—"Cool Thoughts on the Present Situation of our Public Affairs." He instituted a petition in behalf of his cause. Some 3,500 signed it.[18]

What did Assemblyman John Dickinson think of Franklin's proposal? Thomas Penn had been kind to him in London, going so far as to present him at the royal court. Yet Dickinson, owning no particular animus against the family, could see plainly enough the shortcomings of proprietary government. Did that insight qualify him for conversion to Franklin's plan for putting the king in charge? Not as matters played themselves out in the Assembly's internal dispute. In the careful, studious way that would mark all his political interventions, Dickinson came down against the Franklin party—but for reasons that neither faction might have anticipated.

The matter, for Dickinson, rose above the essentially earthbound question, how bad are the proprietors? Not that our young and ambitious lawyer was completely above personalizing a question of right and wrong. Dickinson disliked and distrusted the leader of the Assembly's pro-proprietary faction, Benjamin Chew, a fellow Delaware landowner with whom he had clashed over what the historian J. H. Hutson calls "the distribution of power and place" in the three counties.[19] Not that Dickinson was any fonder of Franklin's partner in the royal government battle, one Joseph Galloway: a man only a year and a half older than himself; like himself, a major landowner born to a Quaker family; again, like himself, ambitious. The two men's paths had not diverged as sharply as they would during the period of intensifying conflict with Britain. Yet temperament and disparate readings of political need already set them apart. The two were destined to become fervent enemies.

Dickinson became almost by default the leader and voice of the tiny party in the Assembly that took the proprietors' side against Franklin. In thus committing himself, he assumed the vast risk of seeming to back rights that the proprietors exercised in opposition to the interests of most Pennsylvanians. *Seeming* is the operative word. Dickinson knew well enough the irregularities that arose from proprietary control. He preferred, nonetheless, to talk of matters that he saw as more important in the large perspective of human affairs. Franklin and Galloway said that direct royal rule, through an appointed governor, would improve Pennsylvanians' lot. Indeed? Dickinson wished to know on what basis his two self-assured colleagues could prophesy with such exactitude. It seemed likelier to him that, imperfect as the order of things might be under the proprietorship, turning the box upside down, emptying its contents on the floor, then refilling it with new ideas and administrative geegaws could badly impair Pennsylvanians' freedoms. He elaborated his position in a speech delivered to the Assembly on May 24, 1764. The speech was long, filled with complex, graceful turns of phrase that required close attention as he spoke. It was also rich with observation and scholarship.

Conscience had compelled Dickinson to speak. "We ought not to aim only at the approbation of men....Let us act so that we may enjoy our own approbation...: that we may deserve the approbation of the impartial world; and of posterity who are so much interested in the present debate." He tried to train his listeners' attention on considerations larger and more enduring than the grievances of the moment. If Pennsylvanians entertained just resentments regarding the Penns' stewardship, "let our resentment bear proportion to the provocation received; and not produce, or even expose us to the peril, of producing effects more fatal than the injury of which we complain." Prudence and good sense ought to reign, not haste and disorder. He quoted Tacitus against men "who despising those things which they might slowly and safely attain seize them too hastily, and with fatal speech rush upon their own destruction." Such a radical attempt to abolish great grievances "ought not *now* to be made." The Assembly should consider the obvious consequences of overthrowing the proprietorship: "The connection between the proprietary family and this Province may be regarded as a marriage. Our privileges may be called the fruits of that marriage, . . . whenever the parents of an *imprudent request* shall be *divorced*, much I fear that their *issue* will be declared *illegitimate*." Whereas the Charter of 1701 accorded the colony "perfect religious freedom," divorce might lead to establishment of the Church of England. A change of government might lead to the quartering of British troops in the colony. Then what?

Of Pennsylvania's privileges he said: "They are safe now; and *why* should we engage in an enterprise that will render them uncertain? . . . Why should we press forward with this unexampled hurry when no benefit can be derived from it? Why should we have any aversion to deliberation and delay when no injury can attend them?" Let go the hold that Pennsylvanians had on their privileges, "and in an instant we are precipitated from the envied height where we now stand." He was unwilling "to run risques in a matter of such prodigious importance on the credit of any man's opinion, when by a small delay, that can do no harm, the steps we are to take may become more safe." The colonists should wait for "some sign of a favourable disposition in the [British] ministry toward us. I should like to see an olive leaf at least brought to us, before we quit the Ark." Nor had enough Pennsylvanians—only 3,500—come out in support of the Franklin petition. What of all the rest? "I should chuse to see a vast majority of them join with a calm resolution in the measure before I should think myself justifiable in voting for it, even if I approved of it."[20]

Eloquently as he might have spoken, keenly as he might have probed the question, a mere handful of Assembly members flocked to Dickinson's standard. Besides himself, only Joseph Richardson, Isaac Saunders, and John Montgomery voted the next day against forwarding the Franklin petition to London for royal approval. (Dickinson's future father-in-law, Isaac Norris, did join him symbolically by resigning the Assembly speakership to avoid association with such a measure.) There was more ado about the matter from Dickinson and his allies, however sparse in number, who drew up and printed their own petition, then circulated it throughout the city, praying that the king "would be graciously pleased, wholly to disregard the said Petition of the Assembly, as exceedingly grievous in its Nature," and unrepresentative of general opinion in the colony.

Of the enemies Dickinson made by his opposition to royal government, far the bitterest was the proud and touchy Galloway, who went after Dickinson's arguments with rhetorical mace-and-chain. Each man was deeply offended at the conduct of the other. On their way out of the Assembly that day, writes the historian Benjamin Newcomb, "harsh words passed between [the two]. They quickly squared off and exchanged blows. Perhaps Galloway got the better of the fisticuffs, or Dickinson challenged him to a duel. Physical violence went no further."[21]

AN AMERICAN BURKE

The value of *no* in political affairs is less celebrated than the value of *yes*, a word that, unopposed, can initiate new trials larger than the old ones. For which reason, *no*—or, as the case may be, *slow*—deserves to be heard and heeded more often. Saying it with conviction can require no more than stubbornness or perversity. Saying it with wisdom, grace, and courage is an activity that approaches art, as with John Dickinson, who gave reasons that slowed, then reversed, the gathering stampede for royal government. Three decades later, Edmund Burke, in England, would make similar assertions respecting the flamboyant passions awakened by the French Revolution. "A spirit of innovation," Burke would write, "is generally the result of a selfish temper and confined views. People will not look forward to posterity, who never look backward to their ancestors." And again: "It is with infinite caution that any man ought to venture upon pulling down an edifice which has answered in any tolerable degree for ages the common purposes of society." In anticipating Burke (who, to be sure, required no prompting from colonial sources), Dickinson linked arms across the years and the ocean waves with the Old Whigs of England, who saw prudent, gradual reform as a safeguard of liberty—who understood that the present builds solidly on the past. Not without cause would the conservative scholar M. E. Bradford call Dickinson an "American Burke." If the two statesmen never met, their instincts meshed subtly. They would stand with the rooted and the tested over against the products of human guesswork.[22]

The good sense Dickinson talked during the royal government controversy converted a number of younger politicians who had supported the Quaker party. Sentiment at large, in this early trial of the people against their king, repudiated Franklin and his wish to repatriate authority across the Atlantic. "What the prospect of royal government actually did," writes J. H. Hutson, "was repel the people, overwhelming numbers of whom viewed it with trepidation; in fact, some 15,000 signed petitions against it, whereas only 3,500 citizens signed in support of it."[23] The whole notion of royal government for Pennsylvania disappeared: a storm reduced to puddles and gray skies.

Dickinson, who had hoped to make an "immense bustle" in the world, would discover that this first great test had strengthened his prestige and influence. Equally to the point, the experience prepared him in some measure for the trials and sufferings soon to come. If he had found esteem during the royal government controversy, he understood, perhaps from the Roman history he read insatiably, how matters might easily have gone the other way. Something of a Roman himself, he understood his duty. "This truth I am convinced of," he had told the Assembly in his speech of May 24,

> that it will be much easier for me to bear the unmerited reflections of *mistaken zeal* than the just reproaches of a guilty mind. To have concealed my real sentiments, or to have counterfeited such as I do not entertain, in a deliberation of so much consequence as the present, would have been the basest hypocrisy.... If *policy* requires, that our words or actions should *belye* our hearts, I thank God that I *detest* and *despise* all its *arts* and all its advantages.... The great reward of honest action is not the fame or profit that follows them, but the consciousness that attends them.[24]

From which powerful maxim we may if we like extrapolate the challenges that lay ahead for John Dickinson in his relations with the formless, perpetually heaving commodity known as "public opinion." The supposedly transcendent political gifts of suppleness in speech and agility in maneuver must have been deposited on doorsteps other than the Dickinsons' the night of young John's birth. He exercised to the fullest, with minimal regard for personal consequences, the freeborn Englishman's right to speak the truth as he understood it, to move and persuade if he could, and otherwise to take satisfaction in duty honorably performed.

THREE

"YOU RIVET PERPETUAL CHAINS UPON YOUR UNHAPPY COUNTRY"

Time's wingèd chariot, streaking high above the human hurly-burly, offers a vivid but, in the end, implausible platform for viewing history. Which is to say, the passage of centuries can make certain events seem utterly right and natural—beyond doubt, beyond questioning. *Of course* they had to take place. It was in the cards, or the mind of God.

Consider the American Revolution. The gorgeousness of the American narrative (with exceptions for slavery and the fratricidal conflict that put an end to it) seems as natural and unforced a proposition as anything one could imagine. Who could ever have doubted that the apron strings tying the mother country to her fractious children must break, so that the march to American power and exemplarity might commence?

In fact, as we know, the parting of Britain and America was for many Americans an event so improbable as hardly to warrant comment—something on the order of cows jumping over the moon. A breach of the old relationship? To what end? In 1763 the British, with colonial help, perfected their goal of driving the French from North America. A great partnership was in the works—English-speaking men and women on both sides of the Atlantic cooperating for the greater good of all. Benjamin Franklin had hoped Pennsylvania's government might be handed over to the Crown. George Washington, during the French and Indian War, had fought under a British flag. Even the relentless John Adams would confess to his wife, Abigail, as late as 1775 that the prospect of "separation" from Britain "always gave me a great deal of grief."[1]

John Dickinson, for his part, wrote in 1766, "Every drop of blood in my heart is British; and that heart is animated with as warm wishes for her prosperity, as her truest sons can wish."[2]

THE DECLARATION OF RIGHTS AND GRIEVANCES

Wars, by nature disruptive, have disruptive consequences: generally unplanned, normally impossible to control. So with the British victory over France in 1763. The war, by greatly expanding British possessions in the New World and ending the competition with France for New World primacy, compelled London to reassess its relationship with the British colonies across the Atlantic, where, for better or worse, things no longer were as they had been. One thing to be noted and weighed was the potency of the colonies, whose population—in 1700 a mere twentieth the size of Britain's and Ireland's, jointly—would by 1770 amount to 20 percent of that total.[3] Some consideration of the relationship between the mother country and her growing children was due, if not indeed overdue.

A prime factor in that reconsideration was, naturally, economic, in the way that economic factors work their way to the top of virtually every human relationship. What were colonial responsibilities to London, and who defined those responsibilities? No means of answering such questions had been worked out. The empire's legal and juridical structure rested on a series of ad hoc decisions that might or might not have inner coherence. For instance, was it fair to the colonies that Britain set the terms on which trade between itself and the colonies took place? It was how the matter had developed over the past century as Britain, by means of the Navigation Acts, contended with the Dutch Republic for supremacy in trade. Was it right that things should remain in that state?

Both parties asked and answered the question in different ways. From the British standpoint it was only fair, in consideration of the protections and markets the mother country afforded, that the colonies should pay a not insignificant share of their upkeep. From the colonial standpoint, it was more than impractical that their British brethren should decide for them what amount was right to pay—such a course impinged on their English right to submit only to those taxes and imposts laid on them by their chosen representatives.

There was surely, as is often the case in human disputes, some right on both sides. Human factors—traditions, rivalries, fears, phobias—intervened to make resolution hard. As did geographical factors: the sheer distance separating London and Bristol, and their home-bred assumptions, from Philadelphia and New York, and theirs. On the American side, loyalty was as much habit as anything else, and habits can be broken when new occasions teach new duties. On the British side, the cares of people, even British people, whom one never saw face to face were not of first magnitude.

The stern logic of the British position manifested itself in Parliament's passage of the Stamp Act in 1765. If the government needed money—and it did—and if the colonies benefited from British patronage and protection—and they did—it was logical to set a price on those benefits. So it seemed anyway to George Grenville, chancellor of the Exchequer, who saw the matter of revenue solely in economic terms. The colonies had money. Why not exact a share of it for imperial purposes? The Sugar Act, which initiated Grenville's program in 1764, raised the price of non-British goods purchased by the colonists and aimed simultaneously at more efficient collection of the revenues the colonials had found it easy to evade. It was only the foretaste of what Grenville believed should be pressed to colonial lips.

The Stamp Act proved a greater shock yet, imposing on the colonies the first direct tax ever levied by a Parliament in which—an increasingly central point—no American voice was heard. The new law provided that papers and legal documents must bear government-issued stamps. Likewise newspapers, almanacs, broadsides, and tavern licenses. The requirement extended even to dice and playing cards. The plan was to raise 60,000 pounds—just one-fifth of the cost of maintaining British forces in America.

In the abstract the design was sound enough: so many stamps sold, so much money raised. All the Americans had to do was play their assigned roles as "customers." They refused, without the slightest show of contrition. In fact, they more than refused; they raged. Down had come orders from London for Americans to be press-ganged into some foreign fund-raising enterprise. Parliament had bluffly demanded the money it wanted from people unused to hearing, far less complying with, such demands—least of all during the stressful economic times that followed the French and Indian War. The government had presumed on the Americans' part an amenability uncharacteristic of people accustomed to clearing land, plowing fields, fighting Indians, and knocking together dwelling places, on their own or with purely communal assistance.

The Stamp Act was an almost matchless example of political blundering and malapportionment of means and ends. If Grenville had expected meek compliance, he encountered the stark reverse. The burgesses of Virginia, who performed their governmental business in sight of the royal arms of England, heard young Patrick Henry obliquely warn his sovereign not to expect much more complaisance from the colonists than King Charles I had received from his Puritan executioners. The burgesses kept a level voice in protesting taxation without representation, but Henry's incendiary words and propositions got out widely. A Middle Temple–educated lawyer from Maryland, Daniel Dulany, made a sensation by publishing a pamphlet in which he argued that this same lack of representation in Parliament meant colonial assemblies enjoyed the sole right to levy internal taxes. The British could keep their hands out of colonial pants pockets.[4]

A few days after the burgesses had their say, the Massachusetts assembly—a body not known for placidity in the face of challenge—proposed that the colonies send representatives to a Congress that would take counsel on the matter and ponder remedies. With the act not even in effect yet, the affray over stamps had turned sharp. Mobs attacked colonial stamp agents and ransacked the home of the lieutenant governor of Massachusetts, Thomas Hutchinson. Merchants commenced what in the nineteenth century and afterward would be called "boycotts" against British goods.

Despite all the outrage, the Stamp Act Congress, which worked from October 7 to October 25, 1765, in New York City, gave off a gentler glow than the fiery assemblages that were to come. Just twenty-seven delegates from nine colonies did the work at hand: less a "congress," in modern terms, than a subcommittee meeting.

Virginia, Georgia, North Carolina, and New Hampshire neglected to participate at all. The Congress kept its tone of voice low and even, its call for restoration of rights nonbellicose. This was in no small measure because the voice that rose above the battle smoke in New York City was that of John Dickinson.

It was a voice forceful and deliberate at the same time—a lawyer's voice, urging that right things get done in the right way. The Stamp Act crisis would highlight Dickinson's grasp of the art of putting a frame around principle so that it might be properly displayed—not as something sterile, bare, disconnected from daily life but rather as a living thing, with real consequences for the living.

The "Penman of the Revolution" is the name that history attaches regularly—almost monotonously—to Dickinson. The phrase is curious for implying, in the word *revolution*, a conscious attempt to pry apart adversaries Dickinson hoped to reconcile. It is apt anyway, in that over the next several years he would write and deliver countless resolutions, pamphlets, petitions, and speeches addressing the fractured relationship between mother country and colonies. Every clash between the contending parties would find him with pen in hand, arranging his research volumes, adjusting his candle, scattering blotting sand across wet ink. To the often thankless task of speaking truth to power—a phrase that originated with the Quakers of Dickinson's own century, the eighteenth—he brought the invaluable gifts of lucidity, balance, and eloquence. Unlike Thomas Paine, he lacked an eye or an ear, as the case might be, for the stunning, knock-down phrase that stayed on the tongue. Still, it was for literary skill, fortified by scholarship and wisdom, that leaders of the prerevolutionary period looked to John Dickinson as they sought to make the case for colonial rights and perceptions.

The perception at New York City was that a loyal and unoffending people had been wronged by their own kinsmen; further, that, if not corrected, the wrong might afford a precedent for future injuries—no one could say what kind or how many. Dickinson was one of three delegates the Pennsylvania assembly had sent to the Congress. He was at the time thirty-four years old. He set his hand to the composition of a set of resolutions—the Declaration of Rights and Grievances—that proved, for all the difficulty of the task, firm and respectful at the very same time, a balancing act worthy of the efforts good lawyers find themselves obliged at times to undertake. Even after the Congress exercised its editorial prerogative, Dickinson's structure, his point of view, and much of his wording remained. The delegates declared that they were "sincerely devoted, with the warmest sentiments of affection and duty to his majesty's person and government," yet saw it as their "indispensable duty" to relay their "humble opinions" regarding "the most essential rights and liberties of the colonists." They were as free as native Englishmen, they held, and wished to make known that "no Tax [should] be imposed upon them, but with their own Consent, given personally, or by their Representatives."[5]

It was true, the declaration went on, that the colonists, owing to "local circumstances," could not be represented in Parliament. Accordingly, "the only Representatives of the People of these Colonies, are the Persons chosen therein by themselves . . . No Taxes ever have been, or can be, constitutionally imposed on them but by their superior Legislatures." The delegates saw the Stamp Act as compromising the ancient right of trial by jury by giving jurisdiction to vice-admiralty courts in revenue cases. Britain herself might justly worry that the new duties, "extremely burdensome and grievous," could render the colonies "unable to purchase the Manufactures of Great Britain." What could the colonists do, considering their duty "to the best of Sovereigns," but ask for repeal of the Stamp Act "and of other Acts for the Restriction of American Commerce"?[6]

The declaration included thirteen resolves all told, not counting the closing request for repeal. It was clear, thanks to Dickinson's authorship, why the colonists wanted what they wanted. The "Rights and Liberties" of Englishmen were at stake—the right of being taxed only with the implied consent that duly elected representatives receive and the right of trial by jury. An Englishman living in Philadelphia or Boston was as much an Englishman as one at home in Barking or Ipswich. Put thus, was not this a matter for Parliament's closest attention?

And the sovereign's, too? Before the Congress ended, Dickinson drafted the petition actually to be laid before the king. Its spirit was the same as that of the declaration. "The inhabitants of these Colonies" were "inviolably attached to the present happy Establishment of the Protestant Succession in your illustrious House, and deeply sensible of your Royal Attention to their Prosperity and Happiness." By their labors in "the inhospitable Deserts of America" (an odd phrase coming from a Philadelphian!) the "Wealth and Power of Great-Britain" had been "proportionably augmented." Their British connection these colonists esteemed as "our greatest Happiness and Security." His Majesty was invited to consider the colonies as "a boundless Source of Wealth, and Naval Strength," provided the "inherent Rights and Liberties of your Subjects here, upon the principles of the English Constitution" became secure. "The invaluable Rights of taxing ourselves, and of Trial by our Peers" were "confirmed by the great Charter of English Liberty." Wherefore his majesty's "faithful subjects" implored their monarch to take their plight into his "Royal Consideration," affording them the relief they hoped he would see as necessary to their case.[7]

It was a high-minded performance, emphasizing what might be won through cooperation rather than what had been lost through blunder. To twenty-first-century eyes, an eighteenth-century petition can seem an exercise in cringing and forelock tugging, its ornamental compliments giving way with reluctance to the business at hand. It bears recalling that in this "cringing" manner, under a dispensation different from our own, things formerly got done—as well the Stamp Act Congress and its penman knew. A decade distant from the comparative insolence of the Declaration of Independence, the Congress said what it believed needed saying, in the tone necessary to saying it.

Nor was that all John Dickinson had to say about the matter. In November, as the Stamp Act went into effect, he published a broadside, speaking more distinctly in his own voice than in the purported accents of a whole assemblage. He urged, in effect, civil disobedience to the act, lest "you rivet perpetual Chains upon your unhappy Country" through setting a "detestable Precedent" for future incursions on colonial rights. A question of freedom was involved. Without the right to be taxed only by their own representatives, Americans forfeited their "Security of Property." Resistance was the logical course. "ROUSE yourselves therefore, my dear Countrymen. Think, oh! think of the endless miseries you *must* entail upon yourselves, and your Country, by touching the pestilential Cargoes that have been sent to you." This was stout stuff— no part of the fearful, nail-biting image later detractors slapped on Dickinson. A loyal Englishman had taken it upon himself to suggest that loyalty could on occasion ask too much.[8]

The following year, Dickinson would make similar claims when challenged by the Committee of Correspondence in Barbados, the British sugar island in the Caribbean's West Antilles. The committee had charged the Americans, its trading partners, with "rebellious" behavior in their lack of "humble submission to authority." What was this?, Dickinson wanted to know. The *"rights essential to happiness"* come from neither kings nor parliaments. "We claim them from a higher source—from the King of kings, and Lord of all the earth . . . created in us by the decrees of Providence, which establish the laws of our nature. They are born with us; exist with us; and cannot be taken from us by any human power, without taking our lives." Here he anticipates (if in more expressive theological language) the tenor of the great Declaration from which he would walk away, but whose viewpoints overlap his own at crucial points. There was a right, said John Dickinson, to be happy. That right depended on the right to freedom, which in turn depended on security of property. This line of exposition led, ineluctably, to the matter of taxation. Surrender property without giving consent? No man could "be secure in his property, who is liable to impositions, that have NOTHING BUT THE WILL OF THE IMPOSERS to direct them in the measure."[9] So much for arbitrary power—a most un-English kind of power, he might have added. A son of the Middle Temple was standing forth for the ancient freedoms Englishmen before him had received from God Himself.

His blood was up now—his British blood. To the mother country he carried his arguments, in a pamphlet also published at home and entitled "The Late Regulations Respecting the British Colonies on the Continent of America Considered." Dickinson wished it to be clear that Britain herself showed the colonists how to behave in the event the Stamp Act duties became burdensome. "SHE TEACHES US TO MAKE A DISTINCTION BETWEEN HER INTERESTS AND OUR OWN. Teaches! She requires—commands—insists upon it—threatens—compels—and even distresses us into it." The colonists, in response, would look to their own resources and advantages, replacing British goods with "manufactures of our own." Why not? The example of the Swiss was pertinent. The "coarse cloaths and simple furniture" they made themselves "enable them to live in plenty, and to defend their liberty." Factories of one kind and another would soon burgeon throughout the American colonies. It could not "be doubted that, before the end of this century, the modern regulations will teach *America*, that she has resources within herself, of which she never otherwise would have thought." To know it, one had only to consider "her restricted, and almost stagnated trade, with its numerous train of evils—taxes, torn from her without her consent—Her legislative assemblies, the principal pillars of her liberty, crushed into insignificance . . . and general poverty, discontent and despondence stretching themselves" over the land.

There was more in this vein: passionate and reproachful. The colonies had stood by Britain during the late war, "their hearts glowing with every sentiment of duty and affection." Look how they were served in return—by punishment they would never have received save for the very military victories they helped engineer over the French. Dickinson found the irony a sorrowful one. Doubtless the greatest irony of all was the necessity of preaching the gospel of English liberty to Englishmen, who ought, of all people, to have the keenest equipment for discerning the approach of tyranny.[10]

"MEN OF FREE CHARACTER AND FREE SPIRIT"

The colonists' case was much more open and shut (as lawyers might say) than Grenville could have foreseen. He found little enough sympathy at home for the course he had thought so logical. The great wartime prime minister William Pitt the Elder, a firm friend of freedom who had been too ill to attend Parliament when the Stamp Act was passed, quickly took the measure of the situation.

This matter was only superficially about taxes; it was really about freedom. Treading the same path as Dickinson, Pitt rejoiced at Americans' resistance to the act. "Three millions of people so dead as to all the feelings of liberty, as voluntarily submit to be slaves, would have been fit instruments to make slaves of the rest." The Stamp Act, said Pitt, "should be repealed absolutely, totally, and immediately."[11]

Practicality as well as principle drove such declarations. The Americans had not waited for Dickinson to measure out words of loyal reproach to the British government. Merchants by the hundreds, in the colonies' major cities, had a hand in the outcome. They ceased buying British goods, pending repeal of the Stamp Act, after the manner of earlier protests against the Sugar Act. Courts—instruments of the law—closed down rather than bend to the exactions required under a single misbegotten, albeit well-intended, law. British merchants, some fearing or facing bankruptcy—Edmund Burke noted "the universal alarm of the whole trading body of England"—added to the tumult with their own pleas for repeal.[12]

It had to be done. Done it was, on March 18, 1766—with a soft, barely perceptible coda whose importance came to wide notice only afterward. On the same day that repeal was effected, Parliament enacted the Declaratory Act. What did the act declare? The power of Parliament to make laws binding American colonists "in all cases whatsoever." If repeal looked like short-term surrender (as how could it not?), here was the answer for the long term. Parliament reserved the right to rise and fight again, at a time and place of its choosing. Pitt himself saw it as essential for "the sovereign authority of this country to be asserted in as strong terms as can be devised, and be made to extend to every point of legislation whatsoever—except that of taking their money out of their pockets without their consent."[13] From these and like considerations grew the painful knowledge that for Britain to be Britain and America America, the two might well have to occupy separate bedrooms in the house of civilization.

The passage of the Stamp Act invited Americans and Englishmen alike to examine the enormous question of how the thirteen colonies were to be governed and led—and where the final authority rested in their affairs. Burke had told Parliament, in supporting Stamp Act repeal:

> The object is wholly new in the world. It is singular; it is grown up to this magnitude and importance within the memory of man; nothing in history is parallel to it. . . . In this new system a principle of commerce, of artificial commerce, must predominate. This commerce must be secured by a multitude of restraints very alien from the spirit of liberty; and a powerful authority must reside in the principal state, in order to enforce them. But the people who are to be the subjects of these restraints are descendants of Englishmen, and of a high and free spirit. To hold over them a government made up of nothing but restraints and penalties, and taxes in the granting of which they can have no share, will neither be wise nor long practicable. People must be governed in a manner agreeable to their temper and disposition; and men of free character and free spirit must be ruled with, at least, some condescension to this spirit and this character.[14]

Already these same men were learning one lesson. It was that one immensely reliable source of the wisdom and judgment necessary for facing up adequately to Burke's challenge was the slender Philadelphia lawyer John Dickinson.

FOUR

"MY DEAR COUNTRYMEN"

WHAT NEXT, THEN?

Stamp Act repeal was a political poultice laid on the injured relationship between Britain and her American colonies. The wound—not so deep as a well nor so wide as a church door—was alarming enough in its own way. It stemmed from an attempt at defining the thitherto undefined, indeed barely definable. The question begging answer was, whose writ ran farthest and largest in the colonies—Parliament's or that of the colonists themselves? Pitt and Burke, friends of the colonists, understood the matter well enough. Sovereignty might have limits—as when the colonists correctly asserted the right not to be taxed without their consent—but it was no purely mythical beast either. With no one in ultimate control, authority devolved upon those with the desire and resources to assert it, as in the black days limned in the Book of Judges, when "there was no king in Israel." At the same time, practical matters demanded consideration. How could Parliament oblige Britain's overseas relatives to help with family chores and maintenance projects, particularly in the large way indicated by Britain's postwar needs? How was it possible even to talk readily about such matters, with three thousand miles of ocean dividing the peoples in question, and making the idea of American representation in Parliament a velleity at best, a fantasy at worst?

As the Declaratory Act made clear, the British were not done with thinking of ways to bridge the gap between theory and practice. Some probing actions were essential, the most important of which proved to be the Townshend Acts of 1767, which laid import duties on glass, lead, paints, paper, and tea. What was this, then—a return to the regimen of the Stamp Act? Measured by intentions, not quite. The chancellor of the Exchequer, Charles Townshend, was one of the grandees who crossed and recrossed the stage on which played the sometimes perfumed, sometimes rowdy spectacle of eighteenth-century British politics. He had come to power with the gout-stricken Pitt, newly elevated to the House of Lords as Earl of Chatham but unable to function fully as leader of the government, which left Townshend to conceive and enact his own political agenda. That agenda happened to include raising colonial revenues to offset cuts in the domestic land tax. The lack of Chatham's steadying hand in the government became apparent when Townshend sought to exploit a point Benjamin Franklin raised during the Stamp Act controversy. Whereas (said Franklin) Americans rejected "internal" taxes, as on stamps, an "external" tax on imports might go down differently. "Might" was more than enough for Townshend, who proceeded to drive a coach and four through a distinction his reasoning powers informed him was "perfect nonsense."

As enacted by Parliament, June 29, 1767, the Townshend duties, meant for colonial defense and broader governmental purposes, were to take effect on November 20. A prudent statesman would have bided his time. "Champagne Charlie" Townshend, a witty and eloquent speaker, was no one's model of prudence. He plunged forward—and met instantly with rebuff. Town meetings in Boston, Providence, Newport, and New York City (the last venue seething over an attempt the previous year to compel an appropriation for the quartering of British troops) reacted sharply. From the colonial standpoint it was time for clear thinking and exposition about Townshend's gambit—not least, about its implications for the future. Forth stepped America's leading spokesman for colonial rights and liberties, as if on cue.

LETTERS FROM A FARMER IN PENNSYLVANIA

"My dear Countrymen," began an unsigned letter in the *Pennsylvania Chronicle* for November 5, 1767.

> I am a *Farmer*, settled after a variety of fortunes, near the banks of the river *Delaware*, in the Province of *Pennsylvania*....My farm is small; my servants are few, and good; I have a little money at interest; I wish for no more; my employment in my own affairs is easy....
>
> Being generally master of my time, I spend a good deal of it in a library, which I think the most valuable part of my small estate....I have acquired, I believe, a greater knowledge in history, and the laws and constitution of my country, than is generally attained by men of my class....
>
> From my infancy I was taught to love *humanity* and *liberty*.[1]

Whereupon John Dickinson, days short of his thirty-fifth birthday, proceeded to examine and declare baseless the constitutional arguments for this latest attempt to tax the colonies without their consent. The character he assumed—that of farmer—was true to type as well as tactically adroit in an overwhelmingly agricultural country. A man with servants and a library was clearly no bumpkin, but the mode of address prepared readers to understand the writer as one like themselves—as, equally clearly, he felt himself to be.

Letters from a Farmer in Pennsylvania electrified the alert, the concerned, the vexed, the angry from New Hampshire to Georgia. For pith and effectiveness, it rises above all other productions of the pre–Tom Paine era, and it deploys even-tempered logic in a manner to which Paine never aspired. The Dickinson who put his hand to composing the twelve letters that would eventually make up the series summoned his "dear Countrymen" to sober thought. An undoubted crisis had begun. The Farmer, from his rural perch by the Delaware River, intended "to convince the people of these colonies that they are at this moment exposed to the most imminent dangers; and to persuade them immediately, vigorously, and unanimously, to exert themselves in the most firm, but most peaceable manner, for obtaining relief."[2]

"Most firm, but most peaceable."

The formulation—preposterous, possibly, in 1776 but attainable with effort a decade earlier—might be called the Dickinsonian essence: the wisdom of a man who understood the delicate relationship between thought and action, words and deeds. A consistency of analysis and approach informs Dickinson's responses to the mounting colonial crisis. He sees what is right; he glimpses danger just as accurately. The pathway between the two—where it exists at all—can be hard to negotiate in the dark. Is there reason not to try? "The cause of *liberty*," the Farmer responds, "is a cause of too much dignity to be sullied by turbulence and tumult. It ought to be maintained in a manner suitable to her nature. Those who engage in it, should breathe a sedate, yet fervent spirit, animating them to actions of prudence, justice, modesty, bravery, humanity, and magnanimity.... Hot, rash, disorderly proceedings, injure the reputation of the people as to wisdom, valor, and virtue, without procuring them the least benefit."[3]

Or, to go at the matter from the opposite direction, arriving at the same destination: "I am by no means fond of inflammatory measures; I detest them.... But a firm, modest exertion of a free spirit, should never be wanting on public occasions."[4]

Courage and prudence went hand in hand. The burning of barns to get at vermin was an occupation highly to be discouraged, as any farmer worth his fall crops should have been able to testify.

"THE CAUSE OF ALL"

Parliament, and Townshend, had made a mistake: that much it was easy to apprehend from the reaction the new taxes brought about. But what kind of mistake? Purely tactical, or something worse?

In the very first Farmer's letter, that of November 5—on the same date, fifty-nine years earlier, William of Orange had undertaken England's liberation from the royal malpractice of James II—Dickinson noted New York's recent unhappy experience with British intervention. The idea behind the 1765 Quartering Act, which trailed the Stamp Act by only two days, was to compel colonial contributions to support the British troops who, as Parliament liked to emphasize, kept them safe. The New York assembly's resistance had resulted in an unsatisfactory political standoff, leading the Farmer to counsel that acknowledging

British authority to compel any sort of colonial contribution would empower Parliament "to lay *any burthens* they please upon us." The cause of one colony thus became "the cause of *all*." It could not be otherwise: "He certainly is not a wise man, who folds his arms, and reposes himself at home, viewing with unconcern, the flames that have invaded his neighbor's house, without using any endeavors to extinguish them."[5]

The Farmer soon arrived at the Townshend Acts, around whose passage and enforcement swirled the great question of law, about which he knew a thing or two. The acts were unconstitutional, as Dickinson saw it. He had examined the whole range of legislation prior to the Stamp Act dealing with colonial trade. Such duties as the laws allowed "were always imposed with design to restrain the commerce of one part, that was injurious to another, and thus to promote the general welfare.... Never did the British parliament, till the period above mentioned [i.e., 1765], think of imposing duties in America FOR THE PURPOSE OF RAISING A REVENUE.... This I call an innovation; and a most dangerous innovation." Once admitted, it could lead to new duties that suppressed colonial manufactures, "and the tragedy of *American* liberty is finished."[6]

A reader expecting the Farmer to thrust a powerful fist into the air and call out, with Patrick Henry, for King George III to caress his royal neck with apprehension was due some disappointment. The Farmer, far from crying out for rebellion, wished to know, "If once we are separated from our mother country, what new form of government shall we adopt, or where shall we find another Britain to supply our loss? Torn from the body, to which we are united by religion, liberty, laws, affections, relation, language and commerce, we must bleed at every pore." The colonists would do well to avoid anger, which only produces more anger. "Differences, that might be accommodated by kind and respectful behavior, may, by imprudence, be enlarged to an incurable rage." Accordingly, "Let us behave like dutiful children who have received unmerited blows from a beloved parent; but let our complaints speak at the same time the language of affliction and veneration." (It was possibly this passage that prompted a twentieth-century historian to regard with a slight sneer Dickinson's "appeals for childlike submissiveness").[7]

The thing might yet be patched up. A lot of patching was necessary, to be sure. On colonial taxation, Parliament was wrong. The Farmer denied that it had a right "to lay upon these colonies any 'tax' whatever.'" An intricate discussion ensued. Taxes, according to English precedent, were *gifts of the people to the crown, to be employed for public uses.* The question, *pace* Franklin and Townshend, was not "external" or "internal" taxes—it was taxation for purposes of revenue, which mode of taxation could not bear legal scrutiny. Such taxation would lead colonial feet further into the swamp: "each new encroachment will be strengthened by a former." Talk not of the relatively small sums that would go for taxation. "*That* is the very circumstance most alarming to me. For I am convinced, that the authors of this law would never have obtained an act to raise so trifling a sum as it must do, had they not intended by *it* to establish a *precedent* for future use."[8]

To long-term principle the Farmer rose. The thing was about money, yes, and about a discrete piece of legislation, as well as a multiplicity of other grievances. But those factors by themselves showed only part of what was at stake. Freedom was at stake:

WHO ARE A FREE PEOPLE? Not those, over whom government is reasonable and equitably exercised, but those, who live under a government so *constitutionally checked and controlled*, that proper provision is made against its being otherwise exercised. The late act is founded on the destruction of this constitutional security. If the parliament have a right to lay a duty of Four Shillings and Eight pence on a hundred weight of glass, or a ream of papers, they have a right to lay a duty of any other sum on either....If *they* have any right to tax *us*—then, whether *our own money* shall continue in *our own pockets* or not depends no longer on *us*, but on *them*. "There is nothing which" we "can call our own"; or, to use the words of Mr. Locke—"WHAT PROPERTY HAVE" WE "IN THAT, WHICH ANOTHER MAY, BY RIGHT, TAKE, WHEN HE PLEASES, TO HIMSELF?"[9]

The Farmer drove his plow deep into what he judged fertile soil. "*Those* who are *taxed* without their own consent, expressed by themselves or their representatives, are *slaves*. We are taxed without our own consent, expressed by ourselves or our representatives. *We* are therefore—SLAVES." How much plainer was it possible to be? Pitt, denouncing the Stamp Act, had used language equally volatile. "It is my opinion," he had said, "that this kingdom has no right to lay A TAX upon the colonies," given that "the *Americans* are the SONS, not the BASTARDS of *England*." Government had overstepped itself, to the endangerment of hard-won, long-established liberties.[10]

It was more than a matter of mere money. The colonists could dig down if they had to and cross the palms of the king's men with silver. They would do so at grave risk to their futures as free men—that was the point. The question was not, the Farmer wrote, "what evil has actually attended particular measures—but, what evil, in the nature of things, is likely to attend them." The nature of things! We had seen already how these fundamental matters played out. The sight was grim. The Farmer dragged out the examples of Spain and Ireland, countries where liberty had died through the illegal exercise of power. He besought his readers "diligently to study the history of other countries. You can find all the arts, that can possibly be practiced by cunning rulers, or false patriots among yourselves, so fully delineated, that, changing names, the account would serve your own times." The "late act of parliament [was] *only* designed to be a PRECEDENT, whereon the future vassalage of these colonies may be established." It was "an experiment *made of our disposition* . . . a bird sent over the waters, to discover, whether the waves, that lately agitated this part of the world with such violence, have yet *subsided*." Only look! Only see!¹¹

Nothing like the Farmer's *Letters* had been published before in America. The fearsomeness of the occasion lent inspiration, perhaps, to an argument that Dickinson conducted at astoundingly different pitches and velocities. Flights of historical disquisition give way to firm chops of the rhetorical hatchet; capitalized phrases send up flares from the midst of gray paragraphs. A production that begins gently enough, with references to books and the comforts of rural life, takes on urgency and excitement with the flipping of every page. Yet the Farmer will never be taken for a man sharpening first his pen, then his sword. Not the least of Dickinson's accomplishments in the *Letters* was that of steering firmly, even ingeniously, between the poles of rage and mere intellectual interest. If he raised his voice—and he did—it was to draw attention, not to slap recruiting posters on tavern doors.

What was the answer, then—the upshot of all this expostulation? The Farmer and the colonists were to "take care of our *rights*." Yes, yes—how? Through vigilance and union, which, pursued, meant success and safety. "Our *negligence* and our *division* are *distress* and *death*. They are *worse*—They are *shame* and *slavery*. Let us consider ourselves as MEN—FREEMEN—CHRISTIAN

FREEMEN." And: "Let us take care of our *rights*, and we *therein* take care of *our prosperity*."[12]

But how were his countrymen to proceed? "You have nothing to do, but to conduct your affairs *peaceably—prudently—firmly—jointly*. By these means you will support the character of freemen, without losing that of faithful subjects—a good character in any government—one of the best under a *British* government." This, "without falling into rage." "You will convince the world of the justice of your demands, and the purity of your intentions." What had happened before, at the time of the Stamp Act crisis, would happen again.[13]

In these final texts, the soaring body temperature cooled at the last moment, the palpitating heart grown regular again. No crackle of musketry? No minutemen? No. To expect that is to misunderstand Dickinson, a man jealous for doing the right thing rightly, which is to say prudently, with minimal destruction to the contending parties and elements. There were means of upholding and advancing freedom apart from the bloodying of noses.

The mind of a born revolutionary—Paine, say—is simple: no angles, no curves. One thing he wants; the rest will somehow take care of itself. A complex mind like Dickinson's—the mind of a lawyer; to some extent, the mind of one conversant with Quaker ideals—is of a different configuration, full of nooks and large rooms alike, and also refuges. It assigns places of honor to loyalties, friendships, and generational ties, to fragile objects needing protection. It finds the call of a bird a lovelier thing than the whiz of a bullet. Who decides when the second trumps the first? As it happens, circumstances often decide—among those circumstances the whizzings back and forth of many bullets at places called Lexington and Bunker Hill.

A TRIUMPH

The Farmer's *Letters* were more than a success. They were a triumph: the right pamphlet at the right moment. "Their impact and their circulation," says Forrest McDonald, "were unapproached by any publication of the revolutionary period" save, to be sure, *Common Sense*. Reprints multiplied. Twenty-one of America's twenty-five newspapers blazed the Farmer's reasonings. All twelve letters appeared that March in pamphlet form. Praises rang out everywhere, even prior to the general discovery of the writer's identity. A Boston town meeting called the Farmer—whoever he might be— "the friend of Americans, and the common Benefactor of Mankind." Toasts rang out in colonial dining rooms and taverns: "To the Farmer!" Once Dickinson was identified as the author, the College of New Jersey at Princeton made him Doctor of Laws. Moses Coit Tyler relates that "on his entrance one day into a courtroom, whither business called him, the proceedings were stopped in order to recognize his presence, and to make acknowledgement of the greatness and splendor of his services to the country." Tyler adds, "Songs were written in his praise."[14]

The *Letters* caused a stir abroad as well. Lord Hillsborough, the British minister in charge of colonial relations, put it to Benjamin Franklin after reading Letter No. 8 that he, Franklin, must have been the author. He meant no compliment to the learned inventor. Hillsborough regarded the Letters, though "well written," as "extremely wild, &c." Franklin, unwilling as he was to concur in all the Farmer's reasonings, arranged for the *Letters* to be reprinted in London to represent the colonists' "general sentiments." Burke— whose mind resembled Dickinson's in many particulars, especially when the topic on the table was prudence—counted himself an admirer. The English radical John Wilkes, who received a copy from the Boston Sons of Liberty, replied that the Farmer had "perfectly understood" the cause of liberty. In Paris, the Farmer was compared to Cicero.[15]

The Farmer had spoken for, likely, the great majority of his fellow Americans—who bridled at interference from abroad but as yet were unwilling to lay a bellows to the fires already lighted. The Dickinson brief for the colonies was strenuous enough in tone, yet it was no bugle blast of resistance. It was English. The English had shown themselves willing to forbear: to wait for amendment before pushing the issue. True enough, even the patient English had overthrown two sovereigns in the preceding century. But their study—more so in 1688 than in 1649—was to restore as quickly as possible that sense of order amid liberty for which the English were unexampled in Europe. The Farmer's *Letters* were in one sense a plea for a grand constitutional solution in the English mode: the fulfillment of possibilities such as James II had upset by insisting on his own way in all things. Might not Parliament back away from the precipice upon properly estimating the harm from stubbornness of the sort that had stirred up earlier parliaments against their sovereigns?

In fact, a new situation confronted both the colonists and the government in London—the growing difficulty of yoking together in the same constitutional arrangement two different sets of Englishmen, millions of them living three thousand miles apart from the rest and claiming rights that were hard to sanctify in the interest of practical, efficient government. Where was to be the center of authority? (Or as Lenin, no one's idea of a Dickinsonian democrat, would more bluntly put the matter a century and a half later: "Who—Whom?" Who sits upon whom? Who gets sat upon?)

Franklin saw the difficulty clearly enough. To his son William he wrote on March 13, 1768:

I know not . . . what bounds the Farmer sets to the power he acknowledges in Parliament to "regulate the trade of the colonies." It being difficult to draw lines between duties for regulation and those for revenue, and if the Parliament is to be the judge, it seems to me that establishing such principles of distinction will amount to little. The more I have thought and read on the subject the more I find myself confirmed in opinion, that no middle doctrine can well be maintained, I mean not clearly with intelligible arguments.[16]

Franklin was beginning to suspect, in his pragmatic way, that matters might not long go on as they had gone prior to the Stamp Act controversy. Which expectation ran counter to the hopes that John Dickinson worked to keep alive.

BOYCOTT

The Farmer's *Letters* intensified the colonists' sense of grievance at ill treatment by the mother country and their desire to have the matter put right. The Dickinsonian strategy of peaceful resistance still had purchase on colonial minds. There seemed but one thing to do under the circumstances: reinstitute the nonimportation policies that had brought Parliament around during the Stamp Act crisis. Over the course of some months, the merchants of John Dickinson's Philadelphia, and of Boston and New York City, put in place agreements that shut down Britain's rich American market for its goods.

Dickinson lent vital support to the boycott movement, his viewpoints clashing once more with those of Joseph Galloway, the Assembly leader who had vanquished Dickinson in their battle over royal government for Pennsylvania. In Galloway, the antiplebeian sentiments of a particular sort of landowner merged with personal resentment of Dickinson to produce a foot-dragging response far less grounded in philosophy than Dickinson's. Into the rising wind of colonial anger, Galloway argued against "rash and premature action." By contrast, Dickinson in May 1768 launched a broadside and newspaper campaign to bring Philadelphia's merchants into the larger nonimportation alliance. By March 1769 the merchants of both Philadelphia and Baltimore had banned the importation of British goods.

Of all the colonies, Massachusetts proved most disposed to take direct action. Its assembly entered into an extended quarrel with the royal governor, and through him Lord Hillsborough, over a circular letter written by Samuel Adams denouncing the Townshend Acts and soliciting proposals for united colonial action. On the Boston waterfront, a mob beat customs officials.

Virginia's House of Burgesses, in May, unanimously proclaimed that the right of taxation rested with the local authorities. The royal governor responded to this constitutional affront by dissolving the assembly. Undaunted, the members repaired to a tavern and voted to ban the importation of all British goods save for paper. At length, all the colonies but New Hampshire fell in line with nonimportation. From 2.1 million pounds in 1768, the value of British imports to the colonies fell the following year to only 1.3 million pounds.

The author of this economic and political mayhem died before its consequences had played out. The minister charged with unraveling Townshend's handiwork—Frederick, Lord North—conceived a plan whereby all duties would be withdrawn save that on tea. Thus he hoped to divide the colonists and conquer them by logic if not force. The king's consent came on April 12, 1770. A new, decisive decade had arrived—one in which the Farmer's counsel would be no less desired than before, yet also one when louder and angrier voices made voices of the steady and the logical sort harder to hear.

FIVE

"IN FREEDOM WE'RE BORN, AND IN FREEDOM WE'LL LIVE"

THE FIGURE OF JOHN Dickinson we have come to know in portrayals of his anxieties and hesitations is a figure austere in bearing, with none of the distinguishing marks beloved of historians: a passion for the bottle or the ladies, crackling wit, musical gifts, hard times, flights of genius, neglectful parents, a whole train of possibilities that by many accountings shape the great and famous. He had neither red hair and a fiddle like Jefferson nor the flowing mane and waggish solemnity of Franklin. All that apparently distinguished him physically from most other Founders was a certain fragility that sometimes kept him away from important occasions, sometimes sent him home early. Contemporaries found him gracious and dignified, as well as immensely learned. No details arrest in the way, say, that Jefferson's alleged caperings with Sally Hemings seem to arrest.

He was at all events a man evidently at home with himself, mindful of how little in life truly turns upon the perfection of political designs. Amid the toil and disruptions of constant standoffs with the British, he sought normal life. Among other things, he wed on July 19, 1770, when he was a well-seasoned thirty-seven years old—one of the wealthiest and most influential figures in all the Quaker colony.[1] Mary Norris, his chosen, was the daughter of the Pennsylvania Assembly speaker, Isaac Norris, who had resigned his post rather than sign the Assembly petition approving Franklin's plan for royal government of Pennsylvania. More signally, Norris had acquired for the State House the future Liberty Bell—symbol of the celebrated document his son-in-law would abstain from signing.[2]

The Norrises were Quaker gentry if such a category had the least shade of meaning. Isaac's father, also named Isaac, had served many years in the Assembly, often in the speakership. He had been likewise mayor of Philadelphia and chief justice of the province's Supreme Court. In 1717 he had built the house in which the family still lived—Fair Hill, "the place," says biographer Charles J. Stillé, "where the happiest of Dickinson's days were passed." Half farm and half county seat, it rivaled in grandeur the estates of Quaker families such as the Logans (a Norris family connection), Pembertons, Cadwaladers (to whom Dickinson was related through his mother), Lloyds, and Whartons—names that retain, even in the twenty-first century, the flavor of dignity and achievement. The house provided an excellent view of shipping in the Delaware River. Likely better from the standpoint of the family's new son, it had "a very good and extensive library—placed in a low building consisting of several rooms, in the garden, and was a most delightful retreat for contemplative study."[3]

Mary Norris, according to her niece Deborah Logan, "had a very sweet and benevolent expression of countenance, a solid judgment, good sense, a most affectionate disposition, the tenderest sensibility of heart, and elevated piety." Certainly nothing in a Charles Willson Peale portrait of the young bride contradicts that assessment. Peale shows us a youthful, delicate lady with dark hair massed atop her head, benevolence written large across her face. She was no classic beauty in the eighteenth-century sense; she was more fascinating than any mere beauty because more inward, more serious in her affections. Dickinson must have rejoiced to find his suit willingly accepted. She was known to him and her family as Polly. The piety of which her admiring relative spoke was, of course, Quaker. Yet the couple, perhaps at Dickinson's insistence—his attachment to the Society of Friends being comparatively faint and his taste for costly ceremony being slight—had a small wedding at Fair Hill, presided over by a civil magistrate. Of the event itself Dickinson asked the local newspapers to note simply, "Last Thursday, John Dickinson, Esq., was married to Miss Mary Norris." He continued: "An account of the expressions of joy shown on the occasion will give me inexpressible pain, and very great uneasiness to a number of very worthy relations."[4]

If wedding Mary Norris enhanced Dickinson's local prestige, not to mention his already considerable means, so marrying him set her and her home squarely at the center of comings and goings of every sort in the feverish days of the early 1770s. The Townshend Acts were dead (save for the tax on tea). Twice Parliament had reached out a hand to receive taxes from the colonists. Twice it had been obliged to withdraw the hand. Everyone on both sides of the Atlantic knew the last word in the matter had not been spoken. Nor could anyone be quite sure who would speak it, or in what it would consist. The two parties to the confrontation over revenue and rights circled each other like boxers, looking to see where opportunity and advantage lay.

Dickinson, in 1770, enjoyed a popularity and acclaim such as could have come to him only through his extraordinary grasp of the right thing to say at just the right moment—a right thing all the easier to applaud for its being said with force, clarity, and richness of expression. The Farmer's *Letters* were truly a tour de force, citing the likes of Montesquieu, Hume, and Clarendon along with Demosthenes, Tacitus, and Coke. Dickinson stood over the arc of European history, disentangling right perceptions from wrong ones, hoping thereby to teach grave lessons. The problem he faced was that of recommending reconciliation to men not predisposed to think of peace and order as the highest goods, men whose blood was up and who saw the other side of the argument as mostly if not entirely perverse. John Dickinson's faith in the English sense of right and justice was large. It rose above mere emotional attachments to English ways, English memories. It was rational, reasonable. The England that merited respect from its overseas sons and daughters was the country whose laws and institutions embodied respect for natural rights. He made no argument for crying huzzah for the king. He did argue for expecting that the king, and those who served him, understood what an Englishman, wherever he lived, was due.

And so the cause of the colonies remained the cause of reconciliation, if more and more shakily as time went on and incidents multiplied. No one—not even John Dickinson—could determine from history the pattern their dispute with the mother country would follow. Never before had there been such a test of the relationships among free men.

"THE LIBERTY SONG"

John Dickinson's quickness and intellect—fortified as they may have been by the ambition he now and again professed—kept him at the center of colonial affairs, as Philadelphia's wealth and strategic location ensured the city constant notice. A pleasant if somewhat deviant achievement in the Dickinson chronicles was a popular song he chanced to write. To speak more strictly, he wrote lyrics that fit a well-known tune and thereby captured the public spirit and imagination. The effect was the same as if he had sat down at the harpsichord one day and summoned every muse within earshot. "The Liberty Song" adds a whole new dimension to already complicated understandings of a complex man.

Colonial backlash against the Townshend Acts was powerful already when, in May 1768, a new British commissioner of customs in Boston seized the sloop *Liberty*, owned by the merchant John Hancock, on suspicion of smuggling. A mob, taking righteous exception, harried the commissioner and his agents out of town, to Castle William, in Boston Harbor. The governor of Massachusetts asked for the succor of British troops based in distant Halifax, New Brunswick (subsequently Nova Scotia).

Inspiration overtook the methodical Dickinson. He wrote verses that were printed first in the *Boston Gazette* on July 18—"a rather clumsy hymn of patriotic duty and enthusiasm," according to Moses Coit Tyler, but one that suited the moment. To the Boston patriot leader James Otis, the new bard of Pennsylvania wrote: "I have long since renounced poetry, but as indifferent songs are very powerful on certain occasions, I venture to invoke the deserted muses. I hope my good intentions will procure pardon, with those I wish to please, for the boldness of my numbers." Dickinson acknowledged that his "worthy friend" Arthur Lee, a member of the puissant Virginia family, had composed eight lines of the song.[5]

The distinguished English composer William Boyce furnished—without, to be sure, advance knowledge or approval—the melody. Boyce in 1759 had written a rousing song, with lyrics by the great David Garrick, that rejoiced in British military and naval successes during the French war. "Heart of Oak," the title of Garrick's song, in foot-patting common time, addressed the British world with patriotic bravado: "Come cheer up, my lads!,—it's to glory we steer, to add something more to this wonderful year." Transmuted by Dickinson's inspiration, Boyce's music now made a different appeal:

> Come join hand in hand, brave Americans all,
> And rouse your bold hearts at fair Liberty's call;
> No tyrannous acts shall suppress your just claim,
> Or stain with dishonor America's name.

> In freedom we're born, and in freedom we'll live;
> Our purses are ready,
> Steady, friends, steady.
> Not as slaves but as freemen our money we'll give.

And so on, through eight more stanzas: defying "swarms of placemen," hailing "the labors that freemen endure." Notably, the lawyer-balladeer never cast down a gauntlet before the feet of the king. A plea for reconciliation rose amid the final swelling chords:

> This bumper I crown for our sovereign's health,
> And this for Britannia's glory and wealth;
> That wealth, and that glory immortal may be,
> If she is but just, and we are but free.[6]

The song called for the merger of principles dear to British hearts: justice married to freedom—indeed, the former a prerequisite for the latter. How odd and disturbing that the world's freest people, with their unexampled passion for justice, should be indulging in a family quarrel over the precise meaning of ideals that all valued and believed in, none more heartily than John Dickinson.

"The Liberty Song," reprinted in nearly as many papers as had published the Farmer's *Letters*, rang out triumphantly all along the western Atlantic. There were parodies and counterparodies. John Adams was delighted; Mr. Dickinson's little production, he said, cultivated "the sensations of freedom." A twentieth-century historian credited the song's author with summing up "more completely than [other contemporary songs] the common elements of contemporary propaganda—slavery or freedom, the sufferings of the first settlers in defense of liberty, the penalties of submission, the necessity for union, and the rewards of victory."[7]

PEACE AND PRINCIPLE

No piece of music, however popular, could annul the political and legal perplexities confronting both sides in the dispute. Although the ministry in London had misunderstood the delicacy of its mission, it proved capable of feints and maneuvers calculated to soften objections the colonists might raise. Lord North had undermined the colonists' nonimportation movement by orchestrating the repeal of all the Townshend duties save the one on tea and allowing the Quartering Act to expire. By July 1771 the movement was dead, even in such cockpits of outrage as Boston and Virginia. Philadelphia, over Dickinson's objections, scuttled nonimportation on September 12, 1770. He saw the merchants, with their commercial motives, as unreliable allies in the struggle to bring the English homeland around to recognition of its duty to Englishmen abroad. "My countrymen have been provoked, but not quite enough," he wrote to Arthur Lee. He was confident that stronger provocation would come in one form or another. When the time came, he expected to lean for support upon "the body of the people for the strength with which to oppose British tyranny"—meaning for the most part "the landholders of this continent."[8] Rejoining the Pennsylvania Assembly in February 1771, he sought passage of a "spirited" address to King George III in behalf of repealing the tea tax. The address the Assembly approved was by his standards a pale thing—the victim of "much pruning" by the House. In October he stepped down from the Assembly. The games to be played in electoral office had begun to weigh on him.

Not yet forty years old, Dickinson was at the height of his personal and intellectual prestige, known and admired throughout the colonies. His youthful dream of making a bustle in life had found partial fulfillment. Fame and an honorary degree from the College of New Jersey (afterward Princeton University) had come his way. His ideas were the stuff of everyday discourse. The bustle he had made with the Farmer's *Letters*, not to mention "The Liberty Song," was responsible in significant degree for checking ministerial ambitions in London, much to the surprise of the ministers in question. An advocate trained in their own country, a member of their own bar, had produced at a crucial moment the arguments that told most persuasively against their cause. To many on both sides of the Atlantic, John Dickinson appeared to understand the English tradition better than the king's own ministers understood it. The *Letters* offered an enduring rebuke to ministerial pride and presumption. They remain, two and a half centuries later, a production whose qualities repay examination. It was something indeed to have done what Dickinson did as the conflict between the ministers and the colonists grew hotter than either could have supposed would be the case.

The moderate (one might say lawyer-like) conduct of John Dickinson—firm but peaceable in methods and intentions—had thus far, and in the main, helped preserve peace and principle alike. The difficulty in the situation lay in pretending—assuming anyone wished to pretend—that the American and British views of their relationship could be reconciled on the basis of fundamental principles. The fundamental principle operative in the atmosphere of the 1770s was the fast-growing incompatibility of those views. "Two opposing theories of [the Empire] had grown up and could not be reconciled," writes the Pulitzer Prize–winning historian Claude Van Tyne. There was, on one hand, the theory of the great British jurist Lord Mansfield that, by Van Tyne's account, "political power, sovereignty, resided at the centre, in Parliament," which exercised authority "over all those British dominions on which the sun never set." There was, on the other hand, the view of John Adams that—Van Tyne again—"Massachusetts is a perfect state, no other wise dependent upon Great Britain than by having the same King."[9] The "irrepressible conflict" that William H. Seward would describe three quarters of a century later as looming over America, due to slavery, hardly provided this country's first glimpse of ideals that grated and ground against each other.

As the decisive decade of the 1770s unfolded, the task inherent in preserving both peace and principle grew more and more burdensome—and the jibes louder and louder at those essaying the task. Their harried number came soon to include the Pennsylvania Farmer himself.

SIX

"THERE IS A SPIRIT OF
LIBERTY AMONG US"

ALWAYS, IT SEEMED, JUST when the gears of the Anglo-American relationship were beginning once more to turn smoothly after distraction and disturbance, sand found its way into the works. Noise and clatter arose; the hum of harmony and reconciliation died away. Tension took the place of the lazy old amiability that for so many decades marked colonial relationships with the mother country.

The "Boston Massacre"—blame for the incident lay more properly, perhaps, with the mob that set out to provoke British sentinels than with the sentinels who fired on their tormentors—disturbed the peace in March 1770, though it failed to set adjacent tinder ablaze. John Adams and Josiah Quincy, as advocates, procured the acquittal of the captain of the guard and six soldiers who had been put on trial for murder. There was no general appetite—not yet—for confrontations likely to produce an effusion of blood. But for other kinds of defiance, some of them aggressively physical, there was an expanding market, particularly in Massachusetts.

On June 9, 1772, eight boatloads of Providence, Rhode Island, men burned a British revenue schooner, raising tensions with Crown representatives who knew a threat to their authority when they saw one. Then there was the business of the East India Company's tea—not as to its quality but rather concerning the duty levied on it, and the meaning of that duty for the future.

RUSTICUS SPEAKS OUT

John Dickinson had argued in the Farmer's *Letters* that a tax on the colonies for revenue was no part of a rightful and constitutional relationship between Englishmen who happened to live on opposite sides of the Atlantic. The tax on tea—preserved by Parliament when it repealed the other Townshend duties in 1770—remained for the Farmer a live and squirming grievance. A matter of principle was at stake. Could Parliament, or could it not, tax the colonists anything for the purpose of raising money? That was the question Dickinson, newly restored to the Pennsylvania Assembly over the disgruntled objections of his old adversary, Joseph Galloway, invited the Assembly to consider early in 1771.

On moving a petition to the king, Dickinson found himself (hardly to his surprise) named to an eight-man committee charged with drafting a plea for relief. As amended and adopted finally on March 9, the petition was no model of what later generations would call straight talk. There was much bowing and sweeping back of coat skirts as the Assembly stepped up to the task of "humbly" requesting "your Royal Wisdom" to consider the Pennsylvanians' "dutiful Supplications." Possibly this was at the instance of Galloway, a man more willing than Dickinson—though their politics had points of intersection—to look the other way when the

British blotted their copybook. Yet the document bore unmistak-able Dickinsonian touches. Retention of the tea tax, the petition said, looked for all the world like a strategy designed to establish a precedent "for repeating such Taxations upon us hereafter." This would never do. "As we cannot, from our Situation, be in any Manner represented in Parliament, your Royal Wisdom will perceive that we can call nothing our own, which others assume a Right to take from us, without our Consent." The Assembly had no wish to assert any new right against the Crown and Parliament "but only to be restored to that which we constantly till of late enjoyed"—namely, the "Privilege" of "making voluntary Gifts of our Property" to the king.[1]

Nothing came of the Assembly's assiduous humility. The tax stayed in the statute books. Worse, an authentic teapot tempest blew in from the East. In 1773 the East India Company—that fabulous set of adventurers who controlled commerce between Britain and the Indian subcontinent—teetered on the edge of bankruptcy on account of its inability to dispose of seventeen mil-lion pounds of tea. Parliament's answer was the Tea Act. Under this dispensation, John Company (as Englishmen commonly called it) could sell its tea to agents in the colonies, paying only the 3-pence-per-pound Townshend duty that had offended Penn-sylvania's Assembly. The company could bypass the middlemen of the colonies and undercut the smugglers whose stock in trade was cheap Dutch tea—no match in quality for the company's product, and soon to become costlier, owing to Parliament's intervention. A better product at lower cost: what a gift to the colonists! Or so Parliament believed. The East India Company found merchants in Boston, Philadelphia, New York, and Charleston prepared to buy and retail the tea on company terms—a half million pounds of it to begin.

Yet the deal went wrong from the start. It was well enough to allow a better, cheaper product onto the market, but there was a principle at stake—one that Dickinson saw at once. A commercial monopoly, noncolonial at that, was going to control tea commerce in the colonies, rendering the colonists mute and obedient customers. The tea-importing merchants outside the East India Company's network were of course enraged, but so also were the potential customers, who began to swear off tea in favor of coffee and chocolate. At a mass meeting on October 16, Philadelphians condemned the Tea Act and appointed a committee to demand that local merchants refuse any dealings with the East India Company. Various affrays over tea ensued at various American destinations—of which the Boston Tea Party of December 16, 1773, is the best remembered and most generously chronicled (an inspiration more than 230 years later for a new American political movement).

Before the pseudo-Mohawks of Boston appeared on board the tea-laden English ship *Dartmouth*, John Dickinson had put the case against the Tea Act in terms more strenuous than he had employed against the Townshend Acts. In a November broadside entitled "A Letter from the Country, to a Gentleman in Philadelphia: My Dear Friend [signed] Rusticus," the Pennsylvania Farmer once more donned his metaphorical smock and essayed a critical look at British policy. His blood was up. The composition's second sentence saw the East India Company addressing its parlous financial situation "by the Ruin of *American* freedom and Liberty!" The company's leaders came in for a verbal thrashing. "They have levied War, excited Rebellions, dethroned lawful Princes, and sacrificed Millions for the Sake of Gain." And much else besides. They saw America now "as a new Theatre, whereon to exercise their Talents of Rapine, Oppression and Cruelty. The Monopoly of Tea is, I dare say, but a small Part of the Plan they have formed to strip us of our Property." The principle, not "the paltry sum of Three-Pence," was what counted. And that principle was nothing less than the right of Americans to that which was theirs.[2]

The deterioration of the British-colonial relationship filled Dickinson with apprehension. As Rusticus portrayed matters, the relationship contained an element of what the twenty-first century would call codependency. "The Happiness and Prosperity both of the Colonies and of *Great-Britain* depend upon an Intimate Union & Connexion." The union depended on freedom as the basis of confidence and affection. To preserve it, "and promote the Happiness and Prosperity of both Countries, let us resolve to maintain our Liberty." The present occasion was indeed an unhappy one. Rusticus yearned "for a Return of the old good Humour, Confidence and Affection, which has subsisted between Great-Britain and this Country, since the first settlement of the Colonies."

The phrase was revealing. It spoke volumes concerning Dickinson's view of the ties that united Britain and her American colonies. A few years later no American but Dickinson and possibly a few others would be willing to speak of shared norms and ancient friendships. Was it necessary that two peoples with so much in common should insult each other's notions of right and wrong? Where did those notions come from in the first place if not from common memories of wrongs righted and rights affirmed? And why could disagreements not be worked out? If Dickinson was, as history seems to teach, a reluctant rebel, his aversion to threats and bluster in colonial dealings with Crown and Parliament arose from his regard for deep realities. Did Parliament's colonial taxation policies transcend colonial rights? Yes—of course! And the remedy was . . . blows? How could that be, and how would it end? With both combatant parties pummeled, weakened, and lastingly alienated? Not if John Dickinson could plant in his countrymen's minds the counsels of restraint, the maxims of united, carefully directed action.

The realism he professed when it came to valuing experience over the speculative made him shake his head at the British government's failure to understand a point that was to him so plain. Could the ministers not see the inconsistency in their own professions? How could they miss the jagged edges of the provocations they seemed set on offering America?

Rusticus, addressing his own countrymen, went on: "Resolve, therefore . . . that no Man will receive the Tea, no Man will let his Stores, nor suffer the Vessel, that brings it, to moor at his Wharf, and that if any Person assists in unlading, landing or storing it, he shall ever after be deemed an Enemy to his Country, and never be employed by his Fellow Citizens. . . . Believe me, my Friend, there is a Spirit of Liberty and a love of their Country among every Class of Men among us, which shew them worthy the Character of free-born *Americans*." The language was strong. It had to be. The other side in the controversy had set its mind on victory. *Conquest* might be another word. In yielding there would be only shame over the loss of liberty. "Rusticus" enjoined steadiness in the face of provocation. "CONFIDE, therefore, in each other. Be firm, be prudent, And may GOD prosper your Endeavours, and enable you to transmit to your Posterity that Freedom derived from your Ancestors."³

Doubtless matters never should have come to this pass. Still, they had. The hand of John Dickinson clutched no firebrand intended for delivery to an untended powder magazine. The summons he sounded was to prudence, restraint, good judgment, tolerance, temperance. Framed by the language of alarm and righteous indignation, the summons could drift away on the breeze.

That was certainly its fate in London. The government of Lord North saw clearly the challenge to its authority; it failed to note the accompanying opportunity to rethink possibly outdated postulates. It proposed decisive action as the "Indians" of Boston inspired acts of resistance in other ports. The idea, embodied in a series of enactments shaped and passed between March 31 and June 2, 1774, was to chastise the people of Boston by closing their port, strengthening the powers of the colony's royal governor, and directing all the colonies—not merely Massachusetts—to quarter British troops in uninhabited houses and the like. Another act—a response to the handling of the Boston "Massacre"—allowed the trial of Crown officials in Massachusetts to be held in Britain rather than before some possibly overheated jury in the Bay Colony. For the four new laws, known generically as the Coercive Acts, the colonists had a name of their own, the "Intolerable Acts."

To this unhappy bill of fare Parliament added a fifth new law. The Quebec Act, enacted the same day (May 20) as two of the acts directed at Massachusetts, aimed to regularize the civil affairs of Quebec, in recently conquered French Canada, by planting there a normal government. In so doing, Parliament gave to Canada land claimed by Virginia, Connecticut, and Massachusetts. The act also granted religious liberty to the French Catholics of Quebec. Meant to obviate resistance to British rule in Canada, the gesture set alarm bells swinging in Protestant American minds as to the prospect of papal influence spreading throughout the continent. Thus far had trust between London and the colonies corroded in just a few years' time.

THE POLITICS OF PRUDENCE

Earlier that spring, Edmund Burke, warm friend of the colonial cause (as well as London agent for New York), had pleaded with his parliamentary colleagues for a lighter hand in dealing with the overseas English. He saw no profit in the stern enterprises of the recent past nor any reason to continue them. He was spiritually at one with John Dickinson as to the futility of invective and provocation in a dispute that might, with patience and unity, be resolved to mutual benefit.[4]

Dickinson was not pleased in the least with Massachusetts's turbulent disposition. He feared the consequences of a single colony's attracting a barrage by standing out too far from home port. To Josiah Quincy of Massachusetts, a more conciliatory soul than Sam Adams (which is perhaps not saying very much), he wrote: "Nothing can throw us in a pernicious confusion but one colony's breaking the line of opposition, by advancing too hastily before the rest. The one which dares to betray the common cause, by rushing forward contrary to the maxims of discipline established by common sense and the experience of ages, will inevitably and utterly perish."[5] Recklessness in behavior never commended itself to an advocate of prudence.

Dickinson, as we have seen, has been identified as "an American Burke."[6] The metaphor is compelling if not easy to sustain at every junction. Both statesmen were deeply read in common law and philosophy. The present they understood as a patch on the past. Modern needs had to be consulted, yes, but always with an eye on the processes by which men had come to their present estate—and on the delicacy necessary to a successful project of reform. To pull up a tree by the roots was an act akin to murder. When it came to roots, the rights of Englishmen, wherever they lived, had the same natural character as trees. Down, down they went into the matter and material of history, as lived by discrete men and women: their stories, their challenges, their failures and successes forming the foundation known as experience. It was a dire thing to forget or ignore experience—always (resorting again to Dickinson's aphorism) a better guide than reason.

John Dickinson and Edmund Burke alike, each one understanding the wonder and complexity of human arrangements, saw simple prudence as a necessary virtue in human affairs, a prop of great commonwealths. Pushing too far a mere theory—the divine right of kings or the power to tax a people unrepresented directly in Parliament—could cause whole structures of relationship to collapse. What was the good of strict logic if all it meant was dust and destruction? Burke was not for baiting the Americans through "metaphysical distinctions." "Leave the Americans as they anciently stood," he counseled, "and these distinctions, born of unhappy contest, will die along with it. They and we, and their and our ancestors, have been happy under that system. Let the memory of all actions in contradiction to that good old mode, on both sides, be extinguished forever."[7] There were echoes here of John Dickinson's prayer for a return of the "old good Humour, Confidence and Affection" that had marked colonists' relationship to Englishmen.

It was not so odd that lawmakers in London could ignore the warnings of a Farmer whose face they had never seen, unless, years earlier, one or two Middle Templars had chanced to come across John Dickinson as he consumed *Coke on Littleton*. It was odder that one of the great minds of the English parliamentary tradition—Burke—could speak without inspiring general acknowledgment of his point. It was a bad time for prophets and the warnings they hoped to convey. The intended audience was starting to shuffle its feet impatiently: louder and louder each day.

CONGRESS

For all Dickinson's fears about Massachusetts recklessness, there was no shutting out the noise from the north. Massachusetts was in no mood to be put off by others' anxieties. In May 1774 letters arrived in Philadelphia from Boston, written by Samuel Adams, John Hancock, and Thomas Cushing and addressed to two local men of moderate outlook in politics—the lawyer Joseph Reed and the merchant Thomas Mifflin, the latter a well-known Quaker. The Boston men hoped Philadelphia would call a public meeting to consider Boston's plight and suspend trade with Britain. There was a subsidiary hope—that the Pennsylvania Farmer could be induced to attend. As Reed would write later, "Mr. Dickinson was in the highest point of Reputation, & possessed a vast influence.... He was of that weight, that it seemed to depend on his being present at the meeting whether or not there should be any measures in opposition to Britain in consequence of it."

A public meeting was a different thing from a pamphlet, whose content and details Dickinson could arrange to his satisfaction. It was little wonder, then, that when Mifflin, Reed, and Charles Thomson—a long-nosed Scots Irishman active with the Sons of Liberty movement—called on Dickinson at home to urge his attendance, they found him (according to Reed) "very distant, cool, and cautious." Though dismayed by the Coercive Acts, he was "equally opposed," writes Charles J. Stillé, "to submission and resistance by force, at least for the present. He preferred to wait until the people should show that they had well weighed the consequences of resistance and were in some measure prepared (which so far they had not shown) to abide by them."[8] It was asking a great deal of people angry and offended, as even the great Burke had implied they ought to be. Could they be made to listen? The visitors wheedled: Was it not true the Farmer's *Letters* had helped dispose their readers to resist parliamentary trespasses? How could the author not rise to the occasion? What if by refusing to attend he invited accusations of timidity, not to mention inconsistency? The three showed how a successful conclusion might be brought off by canny planning. First, Reed would speak "with temper [and] moderation." Mifflin would stoke the flames a little higher. Along then would come Thomson—known by his own account as "a rash man"—to urge "an immediate declaration in favour of Boston." That would leave it to Dickinson to offer counsel better adapted to the moderate and cautious mood of the City of Brotherly Love.[9]

Whatever the argument that clinched his decision, if any did, Dickinson accompanied Thomson to the City Tavern. There Mifflin and Reed waited hopefully in the midst of a crowd numbering two or three hundred. Boston's plea for help and unity was read. Thomson, Reed, and Mifflin played their agreed-on parts, with Thomson lending drama to the occasion by fainting in mid-oratorical flight. Dickinson offset the self-designated hotheads by proposing a special session of the Assembly and formation of a committee of correspondence to offer Boston sympathy and support. "It is agreed on all hands," wrote one participant, Edward Tilghman, to his father in Maryland, "that he spoke with great coolness, calmness, moderation, and good sense."[10]

He might well have. The moment was a dangerous one. Sparks generated in Boston were flying around the colonies. One or more might land on dry straw. That Parliament, through the Intolerable Acts, had gone farther than tradition and prudence warranted was self-evident, except perhaps to Parliament itself. Rebuke, as Dickinson saw it, was essential, but rebuke by itself was just half the story. Britain had to be brought to awareness of the perils that proceeded from its own behavior. Not even Edmund Burke had managed to bring Parliament around. Could the colonists, with their committees of correspondence? (Dickinson, inevitably, was awarded the headship of Pennsylvania's committee.) There was no finding out without trial. Thus by summer the colonies were readying a Congress where Massachusetts men and Virginians and Pennsylvanians could take counsel and plan their next moves. The Congress would meet in John Dickinson's Philadelphia.

SEVEN

"THE FORCE OF ACCUMULATED INJURIES"

PLAINER AND PLAINER IT was becoming that things would not end well, if by "well" one meant what John Dickinson did—namely, the peaceful reconciliation of colonists and mother country without impeachment of colonial rights and liberties. The convening of a pan-colonial Congress might have given serious pause to the government in London had that government not already shown itself prone to overestimate its power.

In Philadelphia, the advocates of patience and conciliation were to sit down with the proponents of urgency and decision. Great questions hung in the air: the Intolerable Acts, the mutinous mood of Boston, the growing disposition among colonists to shut down commercial intercourse with Britain. More than deliberation was wanted at this juncture. Action was wanted, and demanded.

The First Continental Congress, as history would denominate it, assembled on September 5, 1774—not in Philadelphia's State House, where the Pennsylvania Assembly met, but rather in nearby Carpenters' Hall, a stately structure that still stands, used at the time as a kind of guildhall by the city's busy carpentry trade. Joseph Galloway, speaker of the Assembly, had offered the Congress the State House's hospitality. The Congress had declined—reluctant, possibly, to emphasize any connection with a political figure conspicuously slow to fault the British.

The heat of late summer had yet to lift, but the organizers closed the windows and doors of the hall to prevent, insofar as possible, outside intrusion into the proceedings. Fifty-six members from twelve colonies—Georgia had declined participation—eventually shared in the deliberations, under the presidency of Peyton Randolph, member of a family of Virginia grandees. Prior to the royal governor's angrily disbanding the colony's turbulent House of Burgesses, Randolph had been that body's speaker.

Not a few of the large names soon to be linked to the large events of the 1770s and '80s made their way to Philadelphia that summer: the Adamses, John and Samuel, of Massachusetts; John Jay and James Duane of New York; Roger Sherman of Connecticut; the Rutledges of South Carolina, John and Edward; from Virginia, Patrick Henry, Richard Henry Lee, and, just as memorably, George Washington. There were radicals, eager to tell off the British; there were moderates, respectful of the colonies' ties to the mother country yet troubled at the government's uncompromising attitude in respect of colonial rights; there were conservatives, so deeply attached to the British connection and its material benefits that they trembled at any thought of separation. It was not always easy to know the differences among the various temperaments and factions. A conservative like Joseph Galloway could believe, or say he believed, firmly in colonial rights; an advanced proponent of colonial rights, such as John Adams, could consent, reluctantly, to the use of petitionary language he would dearly have loved to strengthen. New England's delegates had decided to suppress—

temporarily—their bent for a break with Britain; more cautious men such as Thomas Mifflin had instructed them that now was no time to press the point.

John Dickinson, for all his high estate in colonial affairs, was for days and days obliged to view the Carpenters' Hall proceedings from outside. Galloway, his frequent rival for ascendancy in Pennsylvania affairs, made sure as speaker of the Assembly that none but Assembly members should represent Pennsylvania at the Congress. This bit of stagecraft neatly excluded Dickinson, a non-member when the Congress commenced its work. Events trumped Galloway's intentions, nonetheless. On October 1 the Philadelphia electorate returned Dickinson to the Assembly. Two weeks later, the Assembly paid Galloway back, replacing him as speaker and naming Dickinson to the delegation at Carpenters' Hall.

In the meantime the Pennsylvania Farmer, whom few outside Pennsylvania had ever met, went anything but unnoticed. On August 31, as the delegates converged on Philadelphia, John Adams saw Dickinson arrive at one lodging place "in his Coach and four beautiful Horses. He was introduced to Me, and very politely said he was exceedingly glad to have the Pleasure of seeing these Gentlemen.... Gave us some account of his late ill Health and his present Gout." It was after this meeting that Adams recorded in his diary the surprising sight—noted earlier in these pages—that the famous Farmer presented: "He is a Shadow—tall, but slender as a Reed—pale as ashes. One would think at first sight that he could not live a Month. Yet upon a more attentive Inspection, he looks as if the Springs of Life were strong enough to last many Years."[1]

Some days later, Adams dined at Dickinson's "Seat at Fair Hill, with his Lady, Mrs. Thompson, Miss Norris and Miss Harrison." He was duly impressed: "Mr. Dickinson has a fine Seat, a beautiful Prospect of the City, the River and the Country—fine

Gardens, and a very good Library." As for his host, "Mr. Dickinson is a very modest Man, and very ingenious, as well as agreeable. He has an excellent Heart, the Cause of his Country lies near it. He is full and clear for allowing to Parliament the Regulation of Trade, upon Principles of Necessity, and the mutual Interest of both Countries." The two met again a few days later. Adams found Dickinson "very agreeable." They would dine together frequently in coming days. Adams saw his new acquaintance, once he was seated at Carpenters' Hall, making "a great Weight in favour of the American Cause."[2]

Whatever his personal impressions of Adams, Dickinson, no diarist, failed to record them. It seems unlikely that he would have consented to such frequent social intercourse had Adams struck him as wild or antisocial. It takes a real feat of the imagination to reconcile the Adams who praised Dickinson's heart and relished his society with the fierce, stick-thumping figure of the HBO series— truculent in debate, dismissive of opposition to his designs. The future president's loving correspondence with Abigail, his wife— by now standard in accounts of the revolutionary period—bathes him in benevolence and public spirit. It obliges less sentimental admirers to suggest that Abigail Adams's "dear friend" was a bit of a pill in his relationships with men of different views on the British question. Joseph Ellis, in a study of Adams's character and traits, notes "the Adams penchant for animosity," framed, as it was, by what Adams saw as his own aptitude for "candor"—"the same brutal honesty that he practiced on himself."

Whatever the case, Adams's accounts of his personal interweavings with Dickinson in the autumn of 1774 have a taste all too poignant to readers aware of the bitter words and accusations that would first mar, then destroy, the relationship of two of the colonial cause's indispensable figures.[3]

STIFFENING RESOLVE

The task facing the delegates at Carpenters' Hall required immense delicacy. How far might they go in asserting their undoubted rights? How far was too far? How best to phrase their objections to British policy? There occurred, as anyone might have expected, powerful swings of mood. First came the decision, on September 17, to endorse a set of resolutions adopted a week earlier by a convention in Suffolk County, Massachusetts—in part a sop to Massachusetts's blazing rage over the Coercive Acts, in part a statement of principle. The so-called Suffolk Resolves declared the Coercive Acts unconstitutional and inoperative—"no obedience is due from this province to either or any part of the acts"—urged the formation of colonial militias for self-defense, and proposed stringent economic sanctions against the British. Despite language affirming the need for reconciliation, the resolves could be taken as a summons to outright rebellion. When news of the Congress's action reached London, men inclined to go easy on the colonists were stunned. No less an eminence than William Legge, Lord Dartmouth, who had succeeded Lord Hillsborough as colonial secretary in 1772, saw the Congress's embrace of the resolves as tantamount to a declaration of war. As the king himself saw things, the Americans had qualified themselves for "blows" in reprisal.[4]

The provocative nature of the Resolves notwithstanding, delegates were ambivalent over whether to attempt a definitive split with Britain. Witness the debate that commenced on September 28 concerning Joseph Galloway's plan for "union" between Britain and her colonies. Union? Was there the barest possibility of such a thing?

A man of property who viewed government as essentially the enterprise of gentlemen, Galloway, one historian writes, "was opposed to the policy of the British ministry, but extremely averse to the rash measures proposed by the Bostonians and Virginians— measures which he believed could lead only to revolution and were so intended."[5] He instructed Pennsylvania's delegates to the Congress "to form and adopt a plan which shall afford the best prospect of obtaining a redress of American grievances, ascertaining American rights and establishing that union which is most essential to the welfare . . . of both countries." The result was an almost breathtaking—at this point in British-colonial relations—"Plan of a Proposed Union between Great Britain and the Colonies." Under this ingenious scheme, each colony would oversee its own domestic affairs. A president appointed by the king, together with a grand council, would become an "inferior and distinct branch of the British legislature." Council and Parliament would share authority over general policy for the colonies. Galloway insisted that nonimportation was too slow a strategy to relieve Boston's plight. Something stronger was wanted. "A state," he declared, "is animated by one soul." In support of his concept, he quoted Pufendorf, Grotius, and Hooker.[6]

For all its untimeliness, there was much about this improbable design to like, not least its potential to define what had never before been defined clearly—namely, the rights and mutual obligations inhering in Britain on one hand and her colonies on the other. That was also, perhaps, the plan's basic weakness. Events had caused the colonists to form a concept of rights they were loath now to adjust. John Jay, James Duane, and Edward Rutledge— respected conservatives all—strongly supported the plan. Rutledge called it "perfect."

In the end, five colonies said yes, and six said no. The Congress proceeded to matters that better suited its appraisal of current realities and never again considered Galloway's design. Before the Congress ended, members voted to expunge this unlikely venture from the written record. Galloway blamed Samuel Adams—a not unlikely guess, given the Bostonians' fury for immediate confrontation.

Dickinson's arrival at Carpenters' Hall in mid-October coincided with the push to conclude business and get on with solutions to the problems at hand. By now the Congress was of a mind to confront the British brethren. A document called the Declaration and Resolves issued forth on October 14. The signers spoke up "as Englishmen . . . asserting and vindicating their rights and liberties," after the example of their ancestors. None of these liberties—including the right of assembly and petition, the right to English common law, and the "free and exclusive power of legislation in their several provincial legislatures"—could be "legally taken from them, altered or abridged by any power whatever, without our consent." They set forth their grievances, with due attention to the Intolerable Acts. They conceded to Parliament (as had the Farmer) the right to regulate external commerce if no revenue should be raised thereby.[7]

With the aim of restoring "happiness and prosperity," the Congress said that the colonies would form a "non-importation, non-consumption, and non-exportation agreement or association." Six days later this ambiguously worded pledge or threat—it was both, in fact—took on specific and impressive shape. Starting December 1, 1774, declared the Congress, America would refuse to import British goods, East India tea, and such items as molasses, coffee, and pimento "from the *British Plantations* or from *Dominica*." The importation of slaves would likewise cease at that time. Nor would the colonies, after March 1, 1775, "purchase or use any East India Tea whatsoever," or any other goods on the nonimportation list. A broad and in many ways touching hint of American resolution in the matter comes through in the pledge to encourage "Frugality, Economy, and Industry" and discourage "every species of extravagance and dissipation," especially horse racing, gaming, and shows. A black ribbon and necklace would suffice for women in mourning, and "we will discontinue the giving of gloves and scarfs at funerals." Violators would be branded "the enemies of *American* Liberty" and punished by publicity and that which later generations would know as boycott. This new regime was meant to last until Parliament should repeal all the specified legislation abridging colonial rights and liberties.[8]

As John Dickinson was aware, there was good English precedent for addressing a wrongheaded or injudicious ruler in this manner. The venerable idea, dating at least from the seventeenth century, was that aggrieved subjects would lay their claims before the ruler, seeking redress in—it was to be hoped—peaceful and efficacious fashion. This was how liberty and order were at the same time to be preserved. The real oddity of the American case was the geographical distance between petitioners and respondents—a distance so great as to delay responses and multiply misunderstandings. The Congress's embrace of the Suffolk Resolves illustrated the impossibility of keeping trans-Atlantic negotiations tactful and deliberate in the age before the invention of the telegraph.

In none of this was there encouragement for Parliament to seek cheap appeasement. By the Congress's reckoning, even so, one more appeal to the king was indicated. It could be that his gracious majesty would cause his "Royal indignation" to fall upon "those designing and dangerous men" whose acts of oppression had "at length compelled us, by the force of accumulated injuries, too severe to be any longer tolerable, to disturb your Majesty's repose by our complaints." The language, the sentiments, unsurprisingly, flowed from the practiced pen of John Dickinson, to whom the Congress, after rejecting Richard Henry Lee's initial draft, entrusted authorship of the petition. The document was meant not to assert new rights but "only to obtain redress of Grievances" through the intervention of a "most gracious Sovereign," "the loving Father of your whole People."[9] There was something discordant in such an approach to a sovereign certain to bristle at a frontal attack on his ministers and their policy—never mind Dickinson's transparent attempt to distinguish the king's malignant servants from the gracious and much-loved king himself.

The petition, however eloquently worded, was certainly one of the most useless productions of Dickinson's career. The king, who received it December 21, 1774, was in no mood to be humbly besought, entreated, implored, etc., etc. Just weeks before, addressing Parliament, he had denounced the "daring spirit of resistance and disobedience to his law" then loose in Massachusetts. Americans who had taken the side of the Bay Colony via the Suffolk Resolves—to say nothing of the Continental Association—were unlikely to find their sovereign's eye resting cordially upon them. The original Lee draft, which Dickinson totally rewrote, might have sufficed as well for the intended purpose.

Little more, if anything at all, came from another document Dickinson crafted under the Congress's auspices. An "Address to the Inhabitants of the Province of Quebec" sought, in the event of a split with Britain, to entice Britain's other North American subjects—the conquered Quebecers—into "a hearty amity with us," for the better securing of their own rights. There was perhaps not much consonance between the political conditions of the French settlers, who had fought the English only a decade earlier, and those of the English colonists to their south, but it seemed to the Congress an enterprise worth essaying. Dickinson's prose is as usual majestic and worth reading on that count alone.[10]

As the Continental Congress broke up, Dickinson judged that the die had been cast. "The Colonists," he wrote presciently to his friend Arthur Lee, "have now taken such grounds that Great Britain must relax, or inevitably involve herself in a civil war, likely in all human probability to overwhelm her with a weight of calamities.... A determined and unanimous resolution animates this Continent, firmly and faithfully to support the common cause to the utmost extremity, in this great struggle for the blessing of liberty—a blessing that can alone render life worth holding." He had labored for peace. He wished for it "ardently." He understood that "delightful as it is, it will come more grateful by being unexpected. The first act of violence on the part of Administration in America, or the attempt to reinforce General Gage this winter or next year, will put the whole Continent in arms, from Nova Scotia to Georgia."[11]

"MODEST, DELICATE, AND TIMID"

On October 24, as the Congress prepared to rise, John Adams confided to his diary growing mistrust of the man he had weeks earlier appraised as a warm friend of his country's cause, and with whom he had dined two days earlier. "Mr. Dickinson," he wrote, "is very modest, delicate, and timid."[12] *Timid* was a serious charge to bring against the author of the Farmer's *Letters*—a man who, like Adams himself, had affirmed the Declaration and Resolves and the Continental Association. The word *delicate* likewise piques curiosity. Had Dickinson's pallor and moderate tone begun to tell against him in the eyes of the ardent Adams? What truly irked Adams, one suspects, was that a man of Dickinson's substance and reputation could dare to differ with him on strategic questions. Could he not see what Adams saw? What was wrong with the man?

Very little was in fact wrong with John Dickinson. He had hopes of a different character from those that Adams brandished. He hoped for liberty with reconciliation, according to the ancient English pattern.

Two of the revolutionary era's most important figures continued at a distance from each other—close by, seldom touching.

EIGHT   ·

"TO DIE FREE-MEN RATHER
THAN TO LIVE LIKE SLAVES"

<hr />

THE GREAT, ENDURING WORK of the Continental Congress lay just ahead. On the topic of the political tempest beating down upon Massachusetts, the colonies had amply expressed themselves. The job now was to wait and watch what might happen next on both sides of the Atlantic.

Before dispersing to their homes as autumn set in, the members voted to reconvene in the spring of the following year—May 10— in the event no constructive response had come from London. On many of the members as they traveled home lay an apprehension that for John Adams and various others was a stimulus to excitement. It was that nothing practical would come of the Congress's entreaties and solicitations, that ahead lay disruptions whose end and consequences no man could foretell but that might—might— leave the thirteen colonies free to pursue their own ends through their own methods, forever.

Nearly three months passed in the measured manner of the pre-electronic age. On January 19, 1775, the ministry of Lord

North invited Parliament's inspection of the Congress's documents and resolves. Lord Chatham (again, William Pitt before elevation to the peerage), with the alacrity for which he was famous as a war leader, saw to the heart of the immediate problem: the heaviness of the hand Britain had laid on the colonies. He commended frankly to the House "the decency, firmness, and wisdom" of the documents the Congress had transmitted, comparing them to the best that any "nation or body of men" had ever produced. As a first step toward reconciliation, he moved to address the colonists' greatest provocation: Britain should immediately evacuate its troops from Boston, Chatham declared. The Lords voted by a margin of 3 to 1 to disregard the counsel of England's recent hero and savior. He tried again. Britain, Chatham said, should, among other things, recognize the Continental Congress and require provincial consent for revenue-raising measures, exacting in return colonial recognition of Parliament's "superintending power" over the empire. Again the Lords refused. Together, the two houses of Parliament declared Massachusetts to be in rebellion—an easy enough deduction from events, however ham-handed as a means of effecting peace.

Chatham had misread the dynamics of the political situation at home—or perhaps, having read those dynamics correctly, was seeking to change them. It scarcely mattered. On February 20, setting forth his own terms for reconciliation, Lord North demonstrated where to his own mind, and the king's, lay the real power over colonial events. A colony that agreed to tax itself for its own defense and for the maintenance of civil government, he proposed, could enjoy exemption from any parliamentary taxes save those intended for regulation.

The prime minister meant to be understood as offering a gesture of conciliation—on the terms, to be sure, of a parent confronted by hardheaded, long-legged sons. The ministry had decided to remind the colonists whose authority in the end trumped whose. Already, on January 27, Lord Dartmouth, the colonial secretary so disconcerted by the Continental Congress's embrace of the Suffolk Resolves, had instructed General Thomas Gage, commander of British forces in Boston, to enforce the full range of parliamentary enactments for the colonies—and never mind the anguished responses that might ensue.

On receiving these directives, Gage commenced preparations for seizing and destroying military supplies stored in the nearby village of Concord.

UNRAVELING

The times were becoming perilous, as John Dickinson, like nearly all his countrymen, could readily see. His proposed marriage of goodwill to courageous firmness was unraveling. Britain had no wish to be lectured, or for that matter entreated, by colonials who almost by definition occupied a secondary station in the imperial pecking order. The Americans found themselves talking louder and louder just to be heard. At the rate things were going, they soon would be shaking their fists in the faces of royal surrogates wearing red coats and wielding muskets. In such an environment, how much could one man, however highly motivated, think to accomplish?

The plight of the many who wished for reconciliation was especially acute in Pennsylvania. No effective opposition to king and Parliament could succeed without the participation of the colony subsequently to be known as the "Keystone State" for its location and leadership. Yet Pennsylvania was far from sure it wanted any part of revolutionary designs. The Quaker factor—though Quakers were no more than a third of the population—was large. Quaker doctrine, with its grounding in pacifism and obedience to authority, was uncongenial to revolutionary enterprises. The Friends "had none of the qualities of revolutionists," according to Isaac Sharpless, a nineteenth-century chronicler of the faith. Dickinson's nineteenth-century biographer, Charles J. Stillé, wrote that they were "essentially a law-abiding people, patient and long-suffering, and not prone to anticipate evil." He added that "passive resistance to wrong . . . was alike their duty and their best policy." They were "not restless, nor noisy, nor quarrelsome."[1]

It all made for a striking contrast with the Puritans of Boston, from whom the Adamses were sprung. The Puritans, whose religious zeal burned with a high flame, had passed on to their temporal heirs a reputation for inflexibility, not to mention outright intolerance. It was possible to ask whether Boston had not brought on itself at least a portion of its problems with the Crown and the ministry. No Quakers had seen the need to dress up as Indians to express their views of the East India Company. Nor had the Quakers much in common, temperamentally, with slave-owning, tobacco-growing Virginians. The Quaker fuse was much longer than fuses to be descried elsewhere in the colonies.

Dickinson rose naturally from, and spoke naturally to, this body of Americans—which earned him some measure of reprobation, from John Adams and others, for letting his supposed religious views trump his love of liberty. The view that Quakerism made Dickinson "timid" (Adams's word) as a champion of colonial rights took hold in his own era and for a long time retained purchase on historians of the period—a phenomenon often described in the modern era as "guilt by association." The Philadelphians who inveigled Dickinson's participation in the local meeting to oppose the East India tea duty were at pains while at his home, they recollected, to quarantine him from his mother and wife, lest the two breathe Quaker pacifism in his ear. The fear was likely fanciful, but Quakers were not to be counted on to sit quietly at the prospect of disquiet. (John Adams seems particularly to have feared the supposed influence of this formidable duo. "If I had such a mother and such a wife," he allowed, with even more than the usual asperity, "I believe I should have shot myself.")[2]

In fact, despite living daily in the midst of Quakerism, Dickinson was not really of the tribe—a well-wisher at most, a friendly observer, a marginal member. The Dickinson family's anger over Quaker attempts to disallow John's half sister's marriage to a non-Quaker helped to define the relationship. The Quakers were unmistakably virtuous folk, but they had a bent for meticulous control of their own. Another factor in Dickinson's relationship to the Meeting was his own religious conscience. His was a spacious and grateful piety, informed by careful and repeated reading of the Bible. Yet commitment to one form of Christian expression over all others was beyond his capability or desire. Dickinson, relates the historian David Jacobson, "remained doubtful about the merits of organized religion and wrote: 'I am not, and probably never shall be, united to any religious Society, because each of them, as a society, hold principles which I cannot adopt.'"[3] He worshipped at least occasionally with the Episcopalians (as Anglicans came to call themselves after the Revolution).

A more sophisticated—and convincing—analysis of the religious component in Dickinson's thoughts on revolution comes from the Pulitzer Prize–winning historian Jack Rakove: "From that unique and complex [Quaker] tradition, Dickinson derived a commitment not to pacifism in the strict sense of refusing to take up arms, but to the moral duty to seek peaceful resolution of all civil conflicts." This disposition, Rakove continues, was reinforced by his attachment to the mother country and his "doubts as to whether a harmonious American nation could ever be built on the sole foundation of opposition to British misrule."[4] The quality of Dickinson's mind, as evidenced in his prolific writings, might alone give title to the view of him as a statesman profoundly attached to liberty and deeply cognizant of reality. To be sure, a boiling, seething age on the lookout for quick, decisive action is unlikely to accord much understanding or sympathy to the nuanced viewpoint, the summons to prolonged and careful reflection.

Even the generally elegant and high-minded Lords and Commons of England were guilty of this deficiency. When Edmund Burke—probably Dickinson's nearest equivalent among parliamentary figures—tried to talk sense to his countrymen, they spurned arguments regarded in a later time as luminous. On March 22, 1775, Burke made one of his greatest speeches when he addressed the topic of conciliation with the colonies. He hoped to head off a ministerial bill requiring New England to trade only with Britain and its West Indian colonies. On and on he went for hours. The bill would not do. Burke knew his colonists: they were devoted not only to liberty "but to liberty according to English ideas and on English principles." As a strategy for dealing with the Americans, "prudent management" was easily superior to force. Freedom itself was at stake. "To prove that the Americans ought not to be free"— Burke did not mean independent, he meant free—"we are obliged to depreciate the value of freedom itself; and we never gain a paltry advantage over them in debate without attacking some of those principles, or deriding some of those feelings, for which our ancestors have shed their blood." He unsheathed here a piece of wisdom famous to the present day: "An Englishman is the unfittest person on earth to argue another Englishman into slavery." Another truth followed: "Magnanimity in politics is not seldom the truest wisdom; and a great empire and little minds go ill together."[5]

The House uttered a metaphorical yawn.

The invitation to look deeper and higher into the affairs of men than anger and resentment allowed was the same invitation, in essence, that Dickinson, on the Atlantic's opposite shore, issued. No more reprehensible, surely, than Burke's attempts to patch up a tattered relationship were Dickinson's consistent calls for restraint in the face of provocation. The highest political duty consists, we repeatedly learn in our own time, in saying to men and women not what they hope to hear but what, for their own good, they need to hear.

The next day, March 23, in a near-miraculous instance of timing, Patrick Henry in Virginia gave Burke's unhearing hearers in London their definitive reply: "I know not what course others may take, but as for me, give me liberty or give me death!"

CRISIS

Events moved at catastrophic speed following the battles (so to call these disorganized if sanguinary affairs) of Lexington and Concord on April 19. Paul Revere had brought the warning from Boston: the British were coming. Massachusetts militia and British regulars aimed, fired, fell. There is no occasion here to elaborate on the narrative. For members of the Continental Congress the date already fixed for reconvening—May 10—might have seemed providential. The Congress had work ahead of it far more urgent than its combined membership could have anticipated the previous October.

The Congress gathered this time in the State House, Philadelphia's most important place of assembly—testimony to the gravity of the occasion. Joseph Galloway, the dethroned Assembly speaker who had wanted to wall off the first Congress from the affairs of the province, would be forced to watch succeeding events from outside, with mounting frustration as the colonists listened more and more carefully to radical rants. New faces of consequence were on hand—John Hancock of Massachusetts; from Pennsylvania, the great Dr. Franklin, as well as James Wilson, John Dickinson's friend and onetime law partner. Again Peyton Randolph was chosen speaker, but shortly afterward, the House of Burgesses in Virginia reclaimed his attention, and he went home, whereupon Hancock took the chair. Randolph's replacement in the Virginia delegation—Thomas Jefferson—was very soon to make his own mark on congressional affairs.

And so to business. Astonishing as it may seem in retrospect, and despite the fervor of the Adamses and others, there was no immediate clamor to declare independence, least of all on the part of the middle colonies of Pennsylvania, New Jersey, Delaware, and Maryland. In New York, John Jay, James Duane, Robert Livingston, and young Gouverneur Morris hoped for a solution short of independence. Jefferson himself hoped for reconciliation.

The majority of these men shared Dickinson's satisfaction with a British connection that underwrote security, property, and at least a close approximation to British rights and liberties. If the British failed to acknowledge the colonial construction of the word *rights*, they might be brought around eventually. Meanwhile, what of that piece of folk wisdom concerning the devils we know? It was late in the day—very late—for reconciliation, yet John Dickinson meant to try for it. He had allies; he had hope; he had a lively mind, and the raw courage to put it furiously to work in time of crisis.

It *was* a crisis. Dickinson had written the previous winter: "The great Point, *at Present*, is to keep up the appearances of an unbroken

Harmony in public measures, for fear of encouraging Great Britain to Hostilities, which, otherwise, she would avoid."[6] *At present.* It all might fall apart, then. Yet there was need to make the attempt.

Ironically, even as Dickinson wrote, Lord Dartmouth was stepping hard on his intentions, signing and hustling into the dispatch bags the orders to General Gage to begin enforcing all the mother country's edicts for the colonies. Following Lexington and Concord, Dickinson wrote to Arthur Lee: "The impious war of tyranny against innocence, has commenced in the neighborhood of Boston." It troubled him deeply. "What topics of reconciliation are now left for men who think as I do, to address our countrymen? . . . While we revere and love our mother country, her sword is opening our veins."[7]

ANTAGONISMS STIRRED

The two important pieces of business that emerged from the Congress in the summer of 1775 both bore the impress of John Dickinson's hand and mind. He did not quite beat down the impatient and pro-independence members; he held them at bay. He found the Congress by and large willing to accommodate his strategy of firmness coupled with temperate talk—a delicate and dangerous game, perhaps, but in 1775 the one that seemed to offer the best prospects for success. "Constitutional reconciliation was Dickinson's goal," writes David Jacobson. "And the weight he placed upon this aim in May of 1775 perhaps indicated that he already feared that the revolutionary movement might go well beyond the attempt to restore the relationship of 1763."[8] In which case . . . ? No one could really say. Even the energetic John Adams lacked prophetic powers.

Whether or not events in Massachusetts could properly be characterized as "war," guns and cannon were blasting away, and men were dying. On June 15 the Congress named George Washington the head of what passed for a Continental army. On July 3 he took command of 14,500 men. Days earlier, the Battle of Bunker Hill, outside Boston, had cost the British—who won, technically speaking—three times the number of casualties the Americans sustained. To cry peace when there was no peace (in paraphrase of Patrick Henry and the Prophet Jeremiah) would have been absurd and contemptible. No one sought such a thing. The two documents the Congress approved in July precariously balanced the compulsions of the moment—decisive action and restraint of the sort that grew acutely painful the longer it went on.

Congress adopted the Olive Branch Petition to the king on July 5. The hope, the expectation, had been that the king himself might intervene in behalf of reconciliation, if, as Dickinson insisted, it was possible to gain his ear. Dickinson was one of five assigned to draft the last words, possibly, that the king would ever hear in behalf of colonial rights. For its language and address, he rightly receives the major share of credit. He had written the previous petition to the king, from which the new one flowed, urgent in tone but dutiful, not to say affectionate, in address. It was a remarkable production, the more so on account of its timing. There had been Lexington; there had been Bunker Hill; American forces had fallen upon, and taken, Fort Ticonderoga. American trepidation over a possible—a likely—breach in relationships was in no sense the invention of a Quaker-bred lawyer from Philadelphia. It was an emotion that racked brains and kept eyes propped open at night from New Hampshire to Georgia. Was it written that the union of mother and children should break apart? Might not some saving formula yet be concocted? That forty-nine members of the Continental Congress put their names to the Olive Branch Petition—John Hancock's at the top; the names of the Adamses, Sam and John, fourth and fifth, respectively; that of Thomas Jefferson still lower—shows better than the document of a year later the anguish and complexity of the moment. By the time the Declaration of Independence came to be signed, jaws and hearts were set firmly. There seemed by then nothing else for it. The Olive Branch Petition—accompanied by the Congress's statement of its reasons for taking arms—was a walk along the edge of a precipice. To jump might prove essential. Then, again, it might not. Who knew for certain?

Dickinson's art, and art it was, kept the tone of the petition balanced between firmness and fidelity. He aimed for a royal audience, furthering the notion that in colonial affairs the king had been ill-served by obtuse and belligerent advisers. And so the American lawyer, speaking by proxy to the English king, hunted in the debris of British-American relationships for evidence of connections a good king would recognize as precious. "Attached to your Majesty's person, family, and Government, with all devotion that principle and affection can inspire, connected with Great Britain by the strongest ties that can unite societies, and deploring every event that tends in any degree to weaken them"—so just one sentence began. Remaining to be read, before another sentence could commence, were 106 words of goodwill and faithful intentions—not to be confused with yelps for mercy. His Majesty's "still faithful Colonists" felt grievances that had "compelled us to arm in our own defence." There was no shrinking from present realities. Colonial loyalty had been outraged by "the irksome variety of artifices, practiced by many of your Majesty's Ministers, the delusive pretenses, fruitless terrors, and unavailing severities, that have, from time to time, been dealt out by them." These varied injuries had filled American minds "with the most painful fears and jealousies." If only the king might graciously interpose his authority "to procure us relief from our afflicting fears and jealousies," all might yet be well and the unity of the empire restored. "Further effusion of blood" might be prevented, whereupon "a happy and permanent reconciliation" might ensue in the hearts of all the English on both sides of the great ocean.[9]

Among these varied English, John Adams could be counted as one of the least susceptible to the prospect of reconciliation. Adams's famous and lasting breach with Dickinson may have had its origin in the duty of putting his signature to notions he found cringing: far too peaceable for the views to which he had lately and decisively come. With his pleas for reconciliation and peace, Dickinson had become a barrier to the vision Adams entertained of an America free to walk its path alone.

The next day, the Congress signed a document more to Adams's taste—though not much more. Very different from the Olive Branch Petition, the Declaration of the Causes and Necessities of Taking Up Arms still bore the heavy imprint of John Dickinson. It furthered the second, complementary part of his strategy.

The job at hand involved justifying resistance as a means of promoting reconciliation. With all its risk and uncertainty, such an approach made complete sense to Dickinson. Americans, and American rights, had been brutalized. Did not the author of the Farmer's *Letters* know this? Did he not know it better perhaps than most? At the same time, breaking with the brutalizers could prove more dangerous than bringing them around through pleas and incentives.

The Continental Congress had originally named a committee to make clear the colonies' reasons for resisting military compulsions. When the committee's work failed to satisfy, Jefferson produced a draft that went in turn to Dickinson, who proposed changes that Jefferson disliked. And so round and round until the drafting committee charged Dickinson with executing one draft more. He worked from Jefferson's draft, adding, subtracting, clarifying, intensifying. When all was done, the words and formulations of the American Revolution's two great stylists lay entwined forever.

Jefferson claimed subsequently that Dickinson had considered his draft too strong and so sought to temper it. What actually happened, as Pauline Maier observes in her account of America's turn to independence, is that Dickinson "had made Jefferson's draft stronger, more assertive, even threatening. He expanded the list of oppressions that, as the document said, forced colonists to choose between 'an unconditional submission to the Tyranny of irritated Ministers, or Resistance by Force,' and inserted a statement that necessity had 'not yet' driven the colonists to disrupt the empire, which raised the possibility of Independence more explicitly than Jefferson had done."[10]

The final document began by reciting colonial grievances at the hands of a Parliament "stimulated by an inordinate Passion for a Power not only unjustifiable, but which they know to be peculiarly reprobated by the very Constitution of that Kingdom," directed toward the "cruel and impolitic Purpose of enslaving these Colonies by Violence." After denouncing General Gage's "cruel Aggression" against the populations of Lexington and Concord, the Congress declared:

> We are reduced to the alternative of chusing an unconditional Submission to the tyranny of irritated Ministers, or resistance by Force. The latter is our choice. We have counted the cost of this contest, and find nothing so dreadful as voluntary Slavery.

Honour, Justice, and Humanity, forbid us tamely to surrender that Freedom which we received from our gallant Ancestors, and which our innocent Posterity have a right to receive from us....Our cause is just. Our union is perfect...[and] the Arms we have been compelled by our Enemies to assume, we will, in defiance of every Hazard, with unabating Firmness and Perseverance, employ for the preservation of our Liberties; being with one Mind resolved to die Free-men rather than to live like Slaves.[11]

It was a stirring production—offset only a little, according to the Congress's grand calculation, by denials of intention to separate from the mother country and a concluding promise to down arms "when Hostilities shall cease on the part of the Aggressors, and all danger of their being renewed shall be removed, and not before."[12]

The same signatures as those of a day earlier were affixed to the declaration: Dickinson's along with the Adamses.' Dickinson liked on the whole the job that had been done. If—he wrote to Arthur Lee—the British were to reject so "unexceptionable" a petition as the Congress had approved, it would "confirm the minds of our Countrymen, to endure all the Misfortunes that may attend the contest."[13] Adams was typically astringent about the whole affair. "In exchange for these Petitions, Declarations, and Addresses," he wrote a few days afterward, "I suppose we shall receive Bills of Attainder and other such like Expression of Esteem and Kindness." He spurned the Congress's plan for an address to the British people, foreseeing in it an unbecoming mix of "Prettynesses, Juvenilities, and . . . Puerilities."[14]

Seeing no reason to treat with countrymen from afar who were killing countrymen close at hand, Adams focused his antagonisms on the Farmer he had praised so recently for love of country and sweetness of conversation. The breach between the two patriot leaders widened and deepened.[15] During the debate on the Olive Branch Petition, Adams, who had spoken in opposition, left the hall on business. He related in his diary:

> Mr. Dickinson observed me, and darted out after me. He broke out upon me in a most abrupt and extraordinary manner; in as violent a passion as he was capable of feeling, and with an air, countenance, and gestures, as rough and haughty as if I had been a school-boy and he the master. He vociferated, "What is the reason, Mr. Adams, that you New-Englanders oppose our measures of reconciliation? . . . Look ye! If you don't concur with us in our pacific system, I and a number of us will break off from you in New England, and we will carry on the opposition by ourselves in our way."

For the shape the supposed tirade took, we have Adams's testimony alone. It is not precisely coin of the realm, reflecting the offended party's viewpoint. Nor is it precisely at variance with hints of a Dickinson temper that could flare at moments of large provocation. There had been, for instance, the physical brush with Joseph Galloway during the row over royal government in Pennsylvania.

By Adams's own account, he replied mildly enough to Dickinson's outburst, saying he expected to comply with the Congress's will—as he trusted Dickinson would do likewise. He added: "These were the last words which ever passed between Mr. Dickinson and me in private."

But hardly the last words they spoke concerning each other, in debate and elsewhere. Adams, the righteous Puritan, ladled out doses of scorn in a letter written July 24 to a friend, James Warren.

He pronounced that "a certain great Fortune and piddling Genius, whose fame has been trumpeted so loudly, has given a silly Cast to our whole Doings." And who could that have been? The matter was too obvious to state. As Adams saw it, Dickinson's interventions in behalf of peace had set back the whole colonial cause, leaving the Americans "between Hawk and Buzzard." The colonists, Adams said, ought to have "raised a naval Power, and opened all our Ports wide; to have arrested every Friend to Government on the Continent and held them as hostages for the poor Victims in Boston"—and *then* opened the door to peace and reconciliation on American terms. Things had instead fallen out poorly.[16]

They were to fall out poorly for Adams himself. A British vessel, at a ferry crossing, intercepted the courier carrying Adams's letter—which the authorities opened, read, and published, in both England and America. One September day, with the Continental Congress back in session in Philadelphia, the spiter and the spited crossed paths. "Walking to the Statehouse this morning," Adams related in his diary,

> I met Mr. Dickinson, on Foot in Chesnut Street. We met, and passed near enough to touch Elbows. He passed without moving his Hat, or Head or Hand. I bowed and pulled off my Hat. He passed hautily by. The Cause of his Offense, is the Letter no doubt which Gage has printed in Draper's Paper. I shall for the future pass him, in the same manner. But I was determined to make my Bow, that I might know his Temper. We are not to be upon speaking Terms, nor bowing Terms, for the time to come.[17]

The future second president of the United States, in his self-engrossment, had lost the friendship, tattered as it might have been by this stage, of the colonies' most learned pleader for American rights. In a public street, John Dickinson had cut him dead. Two men enlisted in the same general—and, as both saw it, righteous—cause had parted company. It was a small portent of the parting soon to come between two whole peoples. Reconciliation might have on its side logic and hope. It was not so easily effected when blood was up, and tempers were short, and vision collided with vision—as Americans and Englishmen alike were soon enough to learn.

NINE

"WAR IS ACTUALLY BEGUN"

NOTHING JOHN DICKINSON DID during a long, meritorious career is so widely marked as one very particular thing he chose not to do. He declined, as history and popular entertainment persist in reminding us, to vote in favor of adopting the most famous document in American history—perhaps in all of Western history since the Reformation. It was an act far less of negation than of courage, as robustly American in its way as taking down musket and powder horn and striding off into the unknowableness of the frontier. There was, by July 1776, not the least chance his arguments would prevail. He made them all the same, then stood aside to await the outcome.

The outcome, as the year began, was not quite preordained, though it was plain that there was no easy exit from the predicament into which anger and emotions had pitched the Anglo-American family. If peace might yet be restored to the household, no one on either side of the commotion knew quite how the job might be done. It would take, on both sides, considerable backing away from positions reasonably held.

Dickinson had anticipated that his Olive Branch Petition might be the last throw of the dice. "Our Rights," he wrote to Arthur Lee, "have already been stated—our Claims made—War is actually begun, and we are carrying it on Vigorously. . . . If they reject this application with Contempt, the more humble it is, [the more such] Treatment will confirm the Minds of [our] Countrymen to endure all the Misfortunes that may attend the Contest."[1] Richard Penn, a former governor of Pennsylvania, carried the petition on the long journey to London. The document reached Lord Dartmouth's hands—more accurately, his pocket—on August 21. Dartmouth passed the petition along to the king. If no formal answer ever reached the colonists, the implied response they received was eloquent enough. Two days after Penn's meeting with Dartmouth, in a speech to the new session of Parliament, George III declared the colonies to be in a state of rebellion. John Adams, had he been standing in the throne room at that pivotal moment, would have nodded with grave satisfaction. He had foreseen as much. He had likely hoped it would happen. It brought matters to a head.

Not that the peace party in the House of Lords (and there was one) was ready to give over the quest for reconciliation. The peers asked for and received on November 7 a reading of Dickinson's petition. The Duke of Richmond called for accepting the document with a view to addressing the colonists' grievances by reversing the various offenses it spelled out. Penn was on hand to assure their lordships that the colonists neither sought independence nor insisted on complete freedom of trade. The audience for such arguments proved a comparatively small one. Handily the House beat down a motion to arrange for conciliation on the terms the Continental Congress had laid down; the majority judged Dartmouth correct in believing "that the softness of the language was purposely adopted to conceal the most traitorous designs." A soft answer, far from turning away wrath, had kindled it. According to a historian of the period, B. D. Bargar, no peripheral questions lurked in the background, such as what right had an extralegal Continental Congress to treat with Parliament and the throne? The nub of the matter was that "there was so little faith and understanding left between Britain and her colonies, that the words of the petition were not believed!" So much for any theoretical middle ground "between complete submission and absolute independence."[2]

What little more remained to be said in the matter, the king himself had already said in his speech to Parliament. His Majesty hoped Americans would see "that to be a subject of Great Britain, with all its consequences, is to be the freest member of any civil society in the known world." About which he was certainly, if abstractly, right. He pledged "tenderness and mercy" to "the unhappy and deluded multitudes" opposing his government's policies.[3] The word *deluded* told the story. The colonists' heads were addled, it seemed. They had only to unscramble their brains and look about them. No more than Adams could understand the British viewpoint could his nominal sovereign appreciate colonial sentiments of outrage.

MILITIAMAN

Dickinson had risked much for the cause of reconciliation. In so doing, he had offended various fellow patriots—the contentious Adams most of all, perhaps. During the crucial summer of 1775, Eliphalet Dyer, a member of the Continental Congress from Connecticut, complained in a letter that Dickinson "is most lately bitter against us and indeavours to make sure every ill Impression upon the Congress against us but I may say he is not very highly Esteemed in Congress. He has taken a part very different from what I believe was expected from the Country in general or from his Constituents."[4]

As to the desires of his "constituents," Dickinson spoke their mind better than many a brooding New England Puritan supposed. Pennsylvania, which from the moment of its birth had aspired to peace in every human context, as yet had no great heart for the contest between colonies and mother country. Philadelphians in 1775, writes Stephen S. Lucas in *Portents of Rebellion*, "were not yet convinced that independence was either inevitable, desirable, or feasible."[5] They hoped the dream of reconciliation might find footing. Dickinson was their man. He not only hoped to close the widening breach between colonies and mother country; he seemed by this stage almost to draw breath in behalf of that pursuit. It was his ceaseless study—virtually the center of his activities. He enjoyed the support, furthermore, of influential Philadelphians, among them James Wilson, the Scottish-born lawyer he himself had trained (who was destined to be travestied in the musical *1776*); the wealthy merchant Robert Morris; and the energetic Anglican clergyman and educator William Smith. "Most," says Lucas, "were affluent, well educated, politically prominent, and had been attached at one time or another to the [interests of the Penn family]....All were alarmed and fearful when faced with what [Joseph] Galloway called 'the ill-shapen, diminutive brat, INDEPENDENCY.'"[6] Most supported the fighting already in progress, hoping that it might belatedly inspire British recognition of the colonies' grievances and thus speed their resolution. The Assembly remained set against independence, instructing the province's delegates to the Continental Congress to seek redress of grievances while rejecting proposals to separate colonies and mother country or to alter Pennsylvania's proprietary style of government. The instructions owed their content and wording, naturally, to John Dickinson.

A commonplace of modern historical commentary is the connection between wealth and political complacency—a point that generally leads to condemnations of patrician stupidity or selfishness. Wealth can indeed make a man conservative—or it can open his eyes to the deceits of money considered as an end in itself. To see protection of property as a motive that eclipses all others in the minds of the propertied is to stretch the point unreasonably far, in the manner of Charles A. Beard a century ago.[7] If the rich are slower to political outrage than are the poor, one plausible explanation is that the rich look from a higher vantage point over the conditions essential to general prosperity. Among the largest of these conditions are peace and the rule of law. The Quaker wealthy would naturally be slower to dabble in revolution, grateful as they were to the Crown and proud of the comparative peace and brotherhood that reigned in Pennsylvania, despite tensions between frontier and city, not to mention old-line Quakers and new-line Presbyterians and Germans.

Rich man's complacency can hardly be called a factor in Dickinson's decision, in the spring of 1775, to accept the colonelcy of a Philadelphia militia battalion. A Quaker military officer? Jane Calvert, a biographer who has focused illuminatingly on Dickinson's Quakerly characteristics, or deficiency thereof, explains that he was not in fact a Quaker. Nor, writes Calvert, was he "a rigid pacifist in the most basic sense of rejecting all violence in every circumstance."[8] An equally sizable question might be, how much did a Philadelphia lawyer of any faith understand concerning military procedures? One thing Dickinson certainly knew was how to sit a horse. He had excelled at it all his life. He had no scarcity of self-confidence either. When, in February 1776, General Washington anticipated a British move against New York City, he looked to Philadelphia militia to help fortify the city. Philadelphia's four battalion colonels vied for the right to command any detachment sent to New York. Dickinson prevailed as the longest-serving of the four. Adams relented long enough in his distaste to commend in a letter to his wife Dickinson's "alacrity and spirit upon this occasion, which certainly becomes his character, and sets a fine example." That very day, Adams related, at an assembly of the four battalions, "Mr. Dickinson mounted the rostrum to harangue them, which he did with great vehemence and pathos, as it is reported."[9]

Besides the prudentially minded, Pennsylvania had its share of advanced, impatient spirits—Joseph Reed, the admired physician Dr. Benjamin Rush, and Dickinson's friend Thomas McKean of Delaware, among them. Their aim was to pry apart the colony and its prudential leadership—at which task the British were of greater help than were the Puritans of Massachusetts. Lord North's plan for conciliation looked more like provocation than anything else. The Congress, before adjourning, rejected the whole affair. It also put on some of the trappings of independent government, naming commissioners to negotiate peace with the Indians and appointing Franklin as postmaster general. On December 23 a royal proclamation declared the colonies closed to commerce from March 1, 1776, forward. A U.S. Navy began to take shape, as did a Committee of Secret Correspondence, charged with sounding out "our friends" abroad with a view to obtaining material aid for the colonial cause.

The Congress named John Dickinson as one of the committee's five members, the other four being Franklin, Benjamin Harrison of Virginia, John Jay of New York, and Thomas Johnson of Maryland. Dickinson's presence on such a consequential body, with such an urgent mission, suggests the widespread approbation he still enjoyed for energy in defense of liberty. No one appraised as timorous or wavering, likely to be frightened by a firefly, or an Adams speech, could have been so much as considered for the position. Dickinson's day was by no means done. Nor had his voice weakened. The problem was that its pitch and timbre were unequal to those of another voice that arose suddenly.

NO MORE WAITING

On January 9, 1776, Thomas Paine barged into the American conversation on liberty by means of a pamphlet published in Philadelphia. Paine, an English immigrant, had lived in the city for all of thirteen months. Never mind; he knew what had to be done. He knew it beyond doubt—that same human commodity to which his brain proved impervious over an active lifetime. *Common Sense; Addressed to the Inhabitants of America* ripples with a moral certainty too clamorous to pass quickly over even today. It may not be one of the profounder productions in the history of Western political thought. It is for all that one of the great pieces of writing ever struck off in behalf of a political cause.

Paine understood his intended readership. He understood as well the power of short, sharp, shocking language. The very title invited assent. The author was giving you truth—plain and rude and harsh. He bade you pay heed. The colonists' formerly gracious sovereign, on the telling of this onetime Norfolk corset maker, suffered linguistic demotion to "Royal Brute of Great Britain." Reconciliation? It was "truly farcical." No greater cause than separation had ever existed. "The blood of the slain, the weeping voice of nature cries, 'TIS TIME TO PART." What was English government anyway but the union of "Monarchical tyranny" with "Aristocratical tyranny." Enough, enough! "O ye that love mankind! Ye that dare oppose not only the tyranny but the tyrant, stand forth!"[10] For all Paine's rationalism in religion, there was an evangelical tone to *Common Sense* bespeaking the kind of warfare that mighty men of God had from time to time preached against the infidel. Another way of hearing him, said John Adams, a man far closer to his viewpoint than to Dickinson's, was as "Emigrant from New Gate [prison], or one who had chiefly associated with such Company."

Without mentioning the venerable name of John Dickinson, Paine wrote the Farmer of Pennsylvania out of the proceedings then afoot between Britain and her colonies. The two had nothing to say to each other concerning the job at hand. "Every quiet method for peace," said Paine, "hath been ineffectual. Our prayers have been rejected with disdain.... Wherefore, since nothing but blows will do, for God's sake let us come to a final separation." A few paragraphs later: "Reconciliation and ruin are nearly related." And later still: "Ye that tell us of harmony and reconciliation, can ye restore to us the time that is past? Can ye give to prostitution its former innocence? Neither can ye reconcile Britain and America.... As well can the lover forgive the ravisher of his mistress, as the continent forgive the murders of Britain." All that Dickinson had worked for, and continued to seek, was, to Paine, mere flummery. The advocates of moderation were weak, prejudiced, or commercially "interested" in the British connection— that, or they liked and admired the British too well, in which case they were likely to wreak more harm than all the other moderate brethren put together.

Dickinson essayed no direct response. What might the classical scholar have said against the bare-knuckle bruiser in defense of a reconciliation policy that lay in ruins? A reply in March by one James Chalmers, of Maryland's Eastern Shore, in a pamphlet entitled "Plain Truth," nevertheless joined Dickinson to Paine's hecklers by means of an ardent dedication. Chalmers praised the great Dickinson's "native Candor and unbounded Benevolence" and invoked his aid in saving the colonies "from impending ruin, under the Syren form of delusive INDEPENDENCE." "Step then forth," Chalmers all but cried out, ". . . and cause the Parent and her Children to embrace, and be foes no more."[11] It was all a bit much. Chalmers did not know his man really well. He appears to have seen Dickinson as a lover more of thrones and empires than of the liberty the Farmer actually saw as the lifeblood of the whole imperial connection. In any case, it was late in the day, with events rushing toward climax. Paine had caught the current mood.

The force of *Common Sense* lay in the decisiveness its language underscored. *Now* was the time. No more waiting; no more fine talk or debate. Now! It was an Alexandrine solution to Gordian perplexities—the kind of solution that tends to fix minds when debate is seen as having droned on too long. No pamphlet—the kind of production at which Dickinson had excelled—could by itself doom the cause of reconciliation. *Common Sense* toughened minds and sensibilities. The number of Americans disposed to hear out the Pennsylvania Farmer on strategic questions, had he wanted to discuss them at length, was fast diminishing: faster still as military engagements between British and American forces—in the South, in Massachusetts, in Canada—spilled larger and larger quantities of blood on both sides.

As the time for final decision approached, advocates of independence, with John Adams in the van, sought to prepare the way by squeezing John Dickinson's Pennsylvania. The colony's Assembly was on record as opposing independence. From a military, commercial, and geographical standpoint, however, Pennsylvania's participation in the revolutionary enterprise was crucial. What to do? Shake up the existing order—that was what. Revolutionize from within.

The projected means was a resolution Adams offered the Continental Congress on May 10, recommending to the various colonies that "where no government sufficient to the exigencies of their affairs have been hitherto established," they adopt "such government as shall . . . best conduce to the happiness and safety of their constituents in particular, and America in general." The idea as applied to Pennsylvania was to undercut the pacific and conservative Quakers, permitting their power to pass into the hands of the colony's Germans, Scotch-Irish, and lower-middle-class "mechanics." A new face for Pennsylvania government could mean new instructions to Pennsylvania's delegates at the Congress.

Adams may have drawn a surprised breath or two on hearing Dickinson give the resolution his support. The Farmer took a lawyerly view of the matter. Pennsylvania already had such a government as the resolution called for, thanks to the Assembly's chartered right of initiating all legislation; thus the resolution had no force there. Flustered, possibly, but hardly outfoxed, Adams prepared a riposte, offering a preamble for the resolution. It called for the suppression of "oaths and affirmations necessary for the support of any government under the crown of Great Britain"— oaths and affirmations such as Pennsylvania required. That would be a new state of affairs indeed, one to which Dickinson would have reacted swiftly—but he had already left for his farm in Delaware. The preamble carried the Congress on a divided vote, with at least one and possibly two abstentions.

The very same day, meeting in Williamsburg, the Virginia convention—successor in authority to the old, prorogued House of Burgesses—cast a yet more momentous vote. The convention asked that the Continental Congress "declare these United Colonies free and independent states absolved from all allegiance to, or dependence upon, the Crown or Parliament of Great Britain." A crowd of Virginians hauled down the British flag from over the capitol. Up they ran, in its stead, a colonial union flag.

TEN

"LET MY COUNTRY TREAT ME AS SHE PLEASES"

FRESH EVENTS RUSHED HARD upon the many enmeshed already in sorting out earlier happenings. The British evacuation of Boston in March 1776, and the failure a month earlier of a plan to invade the southern colonies, had dashed British hopes for a quick end to the rebellion. It had to be acknowledged, nevertheless, that the world's greatest empire was merely warming to the task of maintaining its unity and grandeur. By June 1, a waterborne British force had appeared opposite Charleston. Whatever the Continental Congress meant to do, it had to do quickly—assuming the men who made up the Congress, with their varied notions of the public good, could be brought to one mind.

First there had to be an instrument setting forth intentions. It came in the form of a resolution Richard Henry Lee offered on June 7, on the authorization of the same Virginia convention that only days earlier had asked the Congress for what Lee now proposed. Here they were at last, the stark words behind the stark idea, held up for general inspection. What did Americans want?

Independence? Maintenance of the British connection in some form or another? It was time to decide—past time, indeed.

"BARTER MY CONSCIENCE"

What by now were the prospects for averting what John Dickinson a year earlier had spoken of as "the calamities of civil war"? A mind more otherworldly than Dickinson's (which was itself sharply practical) could not have failed to see those prospects as dim to nonexistent. The truth seems to be that Dickinson himself saw the game was up, the last throw of the dice—the Olive Branch Petition—having come up as a fatal pair of ones. The king's mind and heart, far from melting at the entreaties of his subjects, had solidified. The Dickinson biographer David Jacobson writes, "Sometime in February or March of 1776, Dickinson's attitude shifted noticeably in the direction of attempting independence." His service with the militia might have widened his perspective: drum cadences, flags, uniforms, the general noise of preparation. "He ceased to think that he might avoid independence for the colonies. He conceived of his responsibility as that of preparing his fellow colonists for separation from Great Britain."[1] All that remained was to make the best terms possible for entry into the new state of affairs, where, by definition, disorder was the reigning passion.

The thing, if it was to be done, had to be done right. What did that mean, nevertheless? Nowhere does Dickinson seem to have written down his expectations. His capacious, lawyerly mind, alert to changing realities, played constantly over the changing circumstances. Two peoples—both of them his own—were at war. The fortunes of war were, of course, variable. John Dickinson understood the need to step with care. He desired for one thing to preserve the stability of the charter government in Pennsylvania, challenged by the preface John Adams had succeeded in attaching to the Congress's call for colonial government "sufficient to the exigencies of their affairs."

The preface was meant to close down escape routes for colonies—Pennsylvania being the paradigm—that seemed more than ordinarily prone to nail chewing over the prospect of independence. Pennsylvania's unreliability as an ally took coloration from the Assembly's instructions to its congressional delegation, drafted the previous November by Dickinson himself. The delegates—to their relief in the majority of cases—were to "dissent from, and utterly reject, any proposition (should such be made) that may cause or lead to a separation from the mother-country, or a change in the form of [the proprietary government]." As Charles Stillé puts it, the chief men of the tidy, prosperous Quaker colony "shuddered at the prospect of a revolution, and of war, even if a republic was to be reached only through such a path." It was a state of mind into which Adams and his like could never enter, their own minds having closed firmly on the vision of a destiny lying outside the British orbit. That others might see matters differently from themselves is a possibility that self-respecting revolutionists rarely entertain.[2] This is, of course, how great changes come about: not through delicacy and discretion but through brusqueness and force.

The great change coming Pennsylvania's way was evident by mid-May. The Congress meeting on the ground floor of the Pennsylvania State House was squeezing the Assembly that met on a floor above it, calling into question the Assembly's very legitimacy with its demands (issued legitimately or not) for a new style of colonial government. Below Pennsylvania's leadership level, opinion was turning toward radical, far-reaching measures, as evidenced by mass meetings of independence supporters and by growing defiance of Assembly authority on the part of Philadelphia's five military battalions (one of which had as its colonel John Dickinson). An Assembly that felt the walls closing in chose to reexamine the instructions it had provided its delegates. Adams wrote to James Warren on May 20: "Pennsylvania's Assembly meets this Day and it is said will repeal their Instruction to their Delegates which have made them so exceedingly obnoxious to America in General, and their own Constituents in particular." Notably, perhaps, to John Adams of Massachusetts.

On June 8 an Assembly committee presided over by an appropriately somber Dickinson authorized the colony's delegates to "confer" with their fellow delegates in the interest of "promoting the liberty, safety, and interests of America, reserving to the people of this Colony the sole and exclusive right of regulating its internal government and police." Adams, to say the least, was delighted at what he took to be Dickinson's acknowledgment of the reality that Britain and the colonies no longer were one. "What think you must be my Reflections," he asked Warren, "when I see the Farmer himself now confessing to the Falsehood of all his Prophecies, and the Truth of mine . . . ?" Dickinson, Adams said, must confess that proper preparations had been neglected "in Consequence of fond delusive hopes and deceitful Expectations."[3]

Dickinson, no fantasist, could feel the wall at his back. Faced with a collapse of options when it came to delegate instructions, he had chosen to observe "that law of self-preservation which [God] has seen fit to implant in the hearts of His creatures."[4] He had achieved the most and best he could under the circumstances provided.

Adams's undoubted vanity—not infrequently a mark of the

great—was tinctured by another such mark: realism. He could hear the cannonading to the north. War was on. He knew well enough the large state of things. He had less patience with other realities. The colonies, for instance, lacked a national government and a military force that was more than an assortment of militias. They lacked, furthermore, a friendly association with the only overseas power equipped to take on the British—namely, France. The difference between John Adams and John Dickinson consisted less in respective attachments to English-made liberties than in matters of temperament. Adams was a high-stakes gambler, unafraid to shove in all his chips, counting on his innate ability to brazen his way through any crisis. Not so Dickinson, who wanted to know the moment was propitious, that all things essential to a great enterprise had been taken into account. Both were men of vast moral courage—but courage weighed from different sacks, upon scales differently balanced.

Dickinson's case, in June 1776, was unquestionably a hard one. His ability to slow, if indeed to affect at all, the course of events was fast receding. There remained the necessity of bringing himself through the difficulty with honor intact. One day, at a meeting of Philadelphia battalion officers, he heard the question put as to whether the Assembly had the right to name a brigadier general of militia. One militia officer condemned Dickinson for writing the original delegate instructions and warned that his seeming opposition to independence would cost him the confidence of Pennsylvanians. Dickinson rose to respond, offering words that transcended the occasion:

> The loss of life, or what is dearer than life itself, the Affection of my countrymen shall not deter me from acting as an honest man. These threats that we have just now heard might

have been spared. I defy them, I regard them not—I stand as unmoved by them, as the rock among the waves that dash against it.—I can defy the world, Sir, but—I defy not heaven; nor will I ever barter my conscience for the esteem of mankind. So let my Country treat me as she pleases, still I will act as my conscience directs.[5]

If critics had thought to shame their former spokesman and champion, they discovered they had picked the wrong Farmer. A certain streak of righteousness akin to Adams's own tended to stir when Dickinson thought he heard dereliction or obtuseness imputed to him. Joseph Galloway had found long ago, during the clash over royal government for Pennsylvania, that, in Dickinson's case, a good Quaker upbringing was no natural dam to the overflowings of an aroused spirit.

TO BID ADIEU TO THE BRITISH

June 1776 found Pennsylvania's foremost public men shuttling from floor to floor in the State Hall—from Assembly to Continental Congress and back again. It was an odd, even delicate, juxtaposition of meeting places. The radicals of the Congress, gathered downstairs, needed the complaisance of their important hosts above stairs; large numbers of the hosts saw in the enterprise more danger than honor.

The Congress's first attempt to thrash out the matter of immediate independence, as envisioned by the Richard Henry Lee motion, began in earnest on Saturday, June 8. The debate was not the one-sided affair that legend and popular entertainment may have conditioned us to suspect. Nor was the opposition to the Virginia resolution merely cranky and querulous. There was intelligence in the arguments that Jefferson noted in his account of the day's proceedings. Of Dickinson and other members, he recorded:

> Tho' they were friends to the measures themselves, and saw the impossibility that we should ever again be united with Gr. Britain, yet they were against adopting them at [this] time.... The people of the middle colonies...were not yet ripe for bidding adieu to British connection but...they were fast ripening & in a short time would join in the general voice of America.... Some of them had expressly forbidden their delegates to consent to such a declaration, and others had given no instructions, & consequently no powers to give such consent.[6]

These representatives of the middle colonies suggested that if they held aloof from the cause, their "secession" would weaken it "more than could be compensated by any foreign alliance." As for the Spanish and the French, they might wind up on the British side as easily as the American out of fear that their own colonies might fall prey to an aggressive new nation. Why not take the time necessary, then, to work an advantageous alliance with France?

To John Jay of New York, a prominent moderate, Edward Rutledge of South Carolina wrote with satisfaction at the close of the debate:

> The sensible part of the House opposed the Motion.... They saw no Wisdom in a Declarat. of Indep. nor any other purpose to be enforced by it, but placing ourselves in the Power of those with whom we mean to treat, giving our Enemy Notice of our

Intention before we had taken any step to execute them and thereby enabling them to counteract us in our Intention and rendering ourselves ridiculous in the Eyes of foreign powers by attempting to bring them into a Union with us before we had united with each other.... I wish you had been here. The whole Argument was sustained on one side by R. Livingston, Wilson, Dickinson, and myself, and by the power of all N. England, Virginia and Georgia at the other.[7]

The proponents of the Virginia undertaking had urged, according to Jefferson, that "the question was not whether, by a declaration of independence, we should make ourselves what we are not; but whether we should declare a fact which already exists"; that Pennsylvania and Maryland alone were "absolutely tied up" against independence and that changed circumstances might win their accession to independence; that prospects of military success made the present time a good one for hauling down the British colors. And so on.[8]

The delegates discovered that quick resolution to such a debate was not to be looked for. A three-week recess was declared. On July 1 the delegates would take up where they had left off. During the recess, a committee whose leading members were Adams, Franklin, and Jefferson was to prepare a paper explaining to all the world just what was afoot in His Majesty's North American colonies, and why.

In Pennsylvania the consequences of so many new events were fast coming into sight. The bonds restraining delegates in their views and votes on independence had been relaxed already. A hardly less momentous development concerned the Assembly itself, which shut down for good, disabled by the rise of independence-hungry voters eager to rout out the old proprietors and commence something new. The old charter, the old order, had been good to Dickinson, as well as to many others. Prosperity had abounded, and peace—save, intermittently, on the Indian frontier—had prevailed. It was sorrow to part with the good things of the past, but a new frontier of sorts was in the making. A new breed of pioneers was ready to compel allegiance. As bulwark against immediate independence, Pennsylvania was weakening fast. In the once-imposing fortification, with its turrets and crenellations, widening cracks could be discerned.[9]

THE COMING BREACH

The Congress that reassembled at the start of July bears the most minimal resemblance to its caricature in the Sherman Edwards–Peter Stone musical *1776*—arrogant conservatives in the saddle, lassitude or indifference its general mood. In *1776*, the "conservative" party, animated by John Dickinson, is having nothing to do with the cause of independence. Adams fails one day to turn up. A triumphant Dickinson struts to the fore, leading the naysayers in a merry minuet: "Oh, ye cool, cool conservative men / Our like may never ever be seen again / . . . Let our creed / Be never to exceed / Regulated speed / No matter what the need." The matter could hardly be plainer to these well-bred, well-heeled gentlemen: "Why begin / Till we know that we can win? / And if we cannot win / Why bother to begin?"[10]

Such is theater. History is another matter. The returning delegates were near to making up their minds, assuming many minds remained unmade in early July. Dickinson's Pennsylvania seemed poised for change. Not so the man himself, not at the precise moment that circumstances seemed to have shaped. "It was simply, with him," writes Charles J. Stillé, "as with a multitude of others, a question of expediency, as he himself said afterward."[11] Was now the right time or the wrong? Could one after all really apprehend the difference? The valiant English warrior-parliamentarian Lord Falkland had coined a wonderful aphorism more than a century earlier: "When it is not necessary to change, it is necessary not to change." Whether or not Dickinson had ever encountered this piece of counsel, he had enough of the English common lawyer in him to pause at the precipice, taking the measure of the ground around him. Temperament, and inner understanding, prodded and tugged at him, with pronounced effect—as men like John Adams might have acknowledged, pondering the pull and play of their own highly pronounced temperaments.

The Pennsylvania Farmer had not come around, with zest and zeal, to the cause of independence; yet his services to the cause of liberty were remembered. They made him a potential ally of consequence. The majority of delegates showed some alacrity at overcoming specific objections that he and James Wilson had raised. On June 12 the Congress named Dickinson to a new committee assigned to "prepare and digest the form of a confederation between these colonies." It made sense to consider the means by which deliberate rebels might make common cause. That same day, the Congress established a committee that would "prepare a plan of treaties to be proposed to foreign powers." On it would sit the man who had insisted over and over on the need to secure foreign assistance—John Dickinson, joined by Benjamin Franklin, Robert Morris, Benjamin Harrison, and (a testimony to the priority of great matters over parochial and personal concerns) John Adams.[12]

Stillé suggests that both measures proceeded from a generalized hope among delegates that the great John Dickinson might yet decide to embark on the great journey they purposed.[13] This might be true. There is at least a complementary possibility—namely, that Dickinson's hardheaded arguments helped move particular men from fixation on the coming breach with Britain to consideration of the means by which that breach might become both permanent and glorious. The Farmer had by no means stepped outside the furrow he had for so long plowed so assiduously.

ELEVEN

"THE FINISHING BLOW"

INDEPENDENCE OR NO? THE moment to decide was at hand—or, rather, if John Adams was right, to affirm what already was a fact: that the old days were dead; that it remained to bury them, say a few prayers, and go on to something new.

From the perspective of the future, deaths that have occurred in times past are easy enough to acknowledge. The trick, for the still-living, is to revel in the wisdom that time alone unfolds. The American colonists, in 1776, had British names; they had also British memories. One particular name, that of the king, had been on their lips, in oaths and toasts and prayers, and on documents of all sorts. A flag with intersecting crosses had invited pride and signified protection. Was it time to let all of that go? Many had made the argument that it was time indeed. It was an argument informed by new realities. Whether those realities outweighed competing realities was the question at hand as the Continental Congress met shortly after 9 a.m. on the first day of July in the year 1776.

A Declaration of Independence composed largely, as the whole world knows, by Thomas Jefferson had been presented three days earlier. It spelled out the case the colonists, in the event of independence, would make in behalf of that extraordinary commitment. There might be an informal consensus for separation, but in the best British parliamentary fashion the matter required debate. The colonists had not ceased to be English by virtue of preparing a repudiation of English authority. On Monday the first of July, with Congress sitting as a committee of the whole, under the chairmanship of Benjamin Harrison, John Dickinson arose to make his case. He cannot have expected success. He was too good a lawyer to misread the courtroom. He would say all the same what he thought had to be said.

No secretary recorded and transcribed his remarks, but a twentieth-century historian, J. H. Powell, recovered from a manuscript at the Historical Society of Pennsylvania Dickinson's "abbreviated, cryptic, scrawled" but also carefully prepared notes for the occasion. These, Powell painstakingly brought together in recognizable form. The document is worth careful reading as a corrective to now-sanctified narratives of the American beginning—jubilant bells ringing out over the land, hearts beating as one to the divine promise of a free America.[1]

Dickinson, according to his twentieth-century amanuensis, felt "unequal to the Burthen assigned me" of swimming against the tide. "My Conduct this Day, I expect will give the finishing Blow to my once too great, and (my Integrity considered) now too diminished Popularity." He had nonetheless to "speak, tho I should lose my Life, tho I should lose the Affections of my Country," for "Silence would be guilt." He implored God "to enlighten the Members of this House, that this Decision will be such as will best promote the Liberty[,] Safety and Prosperity of these Colonies." There were those in the Congress, "confiding in our Fortune more boldly than Caesar himself," contending that "we ought to brave the storm in a skiff made of Paper." John Dickinson was not of their number.

Fleeting impressions, instilled by the entertainment industry, and even by historians, that Dickinson was a mass of chewed fingernails and petty anxieties, wiping his brow at every comma, fail to stand up. He might have dissented from the near-universal design of the moment, but he dissented on terms he regarded as purely practical, decidedly nonvisionary. The Dickinson who addressed his peers on July 1 was infinitely more the hardheaded lawyer-statesman, trying to see the matter at hand from all reasonable perspectives, than he was the perspiring pettifogger.

Dickinson's case, for all its pallor against the rich bonfire of Jeffersonian rhetoric, was anything but negligible. America needed French help. Dickinson saw the French as unready yet to come in on the American side. " 'We are not ready for a Rupt[ure],' " he saw them saying. " 'You should have negot[iated] Till We were. We will not be hurried by your impetuosity.' " No aid from foreign powers would come. "It is imposs[ible]," Dickinson said. Let the colonies invite France to determine the right moment for independence. But before that, let us establish our governments and "take the Reg[ula]r form of a State. These preventive measures will show Deliberation, wisdom, caution & Unanimity." The word *caution* betrayed an odd insensitivity to the world of facts. Caution had been tried—on Dickinson's prodding. Where had it brought the colonies?

Still, a war of independence could prove a terrible thing, "carried on with more Sever[ity]. The Bur[ni]ng [of] Towns[, the] Sett[in]g Loose [of] Ind[ian]s on our Frontiers[, has] Not yet [been done.]" The Americans themselves could come "in Bitterness of

Soul to compl[ain] ag[ains]t. our Rashness & ask why We did not settle Diff[erence]s among ourselves, [why we did not] Take Care to secure unsettled Lands....Why [we did] not wait till [we were] better prepar'd [or] till We had made an Exper[imen]t of our Strength."

Where was the foresight in this endeavor? "To escape from the protections we have in British rule by declaring independence would be like Destroy[in]g a House before We have got ano[the]r[,] In Winter with a small Family[,] Then ask[in]g a Neighb[our] to take Us in [and finding] He [is] unprepared."

Dickinson was "alarmed" at the idea of declaring independence "When our Enem[ies] are press[in]g Us so vig[orous]ly, When We are in so wretched a State of Prepar[ati]on[,] When the Sent[iment]s & Design of our expected Friends are so unknown to Us." And when colonial unity was in question. "We should know on what grounds We are to stand with Regard to one another."

And what was to keep a Britain chastened "after one or more unsuccessful Campaigns" from tying up the dogs of war and redressing American grievances? Could the colonies obtain better terms from France? If so, "let us declare Independance. If we cannot, let Us at least withhold that Declaration, till we obtain Terms that are tolerable."

It was not, in certain senses, John Dickinson's grandest oratorical hour. The argument he made was for one thing diffuse: a collection of doubts and warnings rather than a focused vision of what great things might be achieved by delay. There seems to have been in the whole presentation very little of genuine refutation—the kind of thing an English barrister would have wielded against an opponent at the Old Bailey. A likely reason is that the verdict had been settled in advance, and was known to all. Jefferson's account of the proceedings before the recess made clear that opponents of independence—including, specifically, Dickinson—"were friends to the measures themselves," if reluctant to move without greater assurance that the moment was right. To various of these opponents, the matter was becoming clear. The time to go was at hand. Was it? Dickinson wanted to know. A sense of duty appeared to inform the enterprise on which he was launched. Certain things needed saying. Very well—they would be said. Howsoever certain the outcome of the debate, no one could lay it to Dickinson's account that he had been backward in the presentation of important viewpoints. He had, rather, laid on the line his whole reputation for good sense. He had wanted, if possible, peace and, by implication, order and comity—all for the general good. Maybe there was more Quaker in him than he knew at the time.

In fact, the words that drowned John Dickinson's hopes had spilled already from Patrick Henry's lips—"Men cry peace when there is no peace."

Adams was there of course, listening with care. Of what he had heard he would write, with a little more graciousness than was his wont in dealings with Dickinson:

> He had prepared himself apparently with great labor and ardent zeal, in a speech of great length, and with all his eloquence, he combined together all that had been written in pamphlets and newspapers and all that had from time to time been said in Congress by himself and others. He conducted the debate not only with great ingenuity and elegance, but with equal politeness and candor, and was answered in the same spirit.[2]

He was answered, as it happened, by Adams—who noted in his *Autobiography* that he began by disdaining any need for pleas to the divinities favored by classical orators. "The question before me appeared so simple, that I had confidence enough in the plain understanding and common sense that had been given me, to believe that I could answer, to the satisfaction of the House, all the arguments which had been produced, notwithstanding the abilities which had been displayed, and the eloquence with which they had been enforced." No more than Dickinson did Adams have anything novel to say. He had said it all before, and it was time for the colonies to go—to depart the empire. Just before the vote, New Jersey's freshly arrived delegates begged to hear the arguments rehearsed for their benefit. Adams obliged. He "summed up the Reasons, Objections, and Answers, in as concise a manner as I could." He knew them by heart.[3]

A TIME TO CHOOSE

The first vote on the Lee resolution came shortly afterward, with the Congress still sitting in committee. Pennsylvania and South Carolina said no, the former by a single vote. The Delaware delegates split. The delegates from New York abstained, in accordance with instructions from their provincial congress. Rutledge of South Carolina was beginning, all the same, to shift his ground. He asked for a vote the next day on grounds that his delegation might go along for the sake of unanimity.

What, then, of Pennsylvania, and of John Dickinson? Would he stand athwart the proceedings for so long as he thought it essential? The HBO series on John Adams represents Adams as visiting a pale and wigless Dickinson the night before the crucial vote, coaxing him to stand aside and let destiny have its way. No such visit took place. A man who had chosen to throw away his "once too great" popularity had no trouble forming his own conceptions of duty and the public interest. When the Congress convened on July 2, two dissenters from the Lee resolution were discovered absent from the Pennsylvania delegation. They were Robert Morris, the opulent merchant, and John Dickinson. Pennsylvania's 4–3 vote the previous day against the resolution became a 3–2 vote in favor.[4] South Carolina switched to the affirmative. Delaware's split having healed, that colony, too, voted for independence. New York abstained once more, according to legislative instructions. Twelve colonies stood together at last for the new liberty they saw as their undoubted right.

Where Dickinson went during the night of July 1–2 is unrecorded. Likely he remained in his own home. It would be romantic to suppose him, in a fever of anxiety, walking the streets of Philadelphia, staring deep into the Delaware River. Such fancies are for screenwriters to contrive, in the way others of their profession have imagined the historic doings of July 1776.

A CHARGED ATMOSPHERE

Two days after the vote, the Congress approved Thomas Jefferson's declaration—a document concerning which Forrest McDonald makes an intriguing point. To wit: "If Dickinson had swallowed his scruples and voted for independence, it is probable that he, not Jefferson, would have been chosen to write the Declaration of Independence. We can only speculate as to what a Dickinsonian Declaration would have said, but it seems likely that it would have been based upon English constitutional history rather than, as was Jefferson's, upon natural-rights theory—with vastly different implications."[5]

Vastly different indeed. Dickinson's thought rested upon a foundation of traditional, inherited rights—laid down and reinforced with pain and care over long centuries of English, and Christian, history. He believed in the God-given character of rights, but the rights in immediate dispute were those of Englishmen. For the right to trial by jury, habeas corpus, speech, assembly, etc. (not to mention "no taxation without representation"), Englishmen had struggled and striven. Some had died. Such rights were real; tangible; provable, as one might say; different in kind and quality from the abstract rights asserted under the influence of rationalism and the Enlightenment. Dickinson "belonged to the party of memory," as M. E. Bradford acutely phrased it.[6]

Dickinson's argument for prudence in defense of English rights was necessarily enacted in a charged atmosphere, in which ideas and emotions flashed faster before men's eyes than did their tamer cousins, memories. In this charged atmosphere, some of liberty's appointed defenders—members of Parliament—deserved as much censure as any of the kings their forebears resisted. This went for the king as well, whose rebuke from Patrick Henry—"Caesar had his Brutus, Charles the First his Cromwell. . . . And George III may profit from their example"—had more than mere rhetorical flash to recommend it. It was a kind of constitutional lesson in miniature. Burke, whom Dickinson resembled in so many respects, had understood the colonists' grievances as well as Dickinson; he had failed to convince those who needed convincing—that was all. A failure of memory, and of rightful allegiances, was at the heart of the problem that Burke and Dickinson addressed. Those whose job it was to remember, forgot. And, accordingly, lost an empire.

PRUDENCE IN THE HEAT OF PASSION

Dickinson recovered in time from the blow to his once too great popularity. He was too imposing a figure for his fellow Americans to cast into outer darkness. Nor had he made unnecessary trouble for the American cause. When he saw his own cause rebuffed, he withdrew, leaving the majority to do what it had decided upon. He did so not without grief and something, perhaps, very like temporary despair.

There is psychological intensity in Dickinson's wrestlings with the consequences of his stand in Philadelphia: now anger; now displays of satisfaction and wounded innocence; now forgiveness and understanding. There is even ribald byplay. "No youthful Lover," he assured his friend Charles Thomson, secretary of the Congress, "ever stript off his Cloathes to step into Bed to his blooming and beautiful Bride with more Delight than I have cast off my Popularity."[7] If the image was incongruous, born as it was in the mind of a great advocate and Christian moralist, so also it overstated Dickinson's supposed satisfaction with rejection and reproach. The theme of willing sacrifice was one he sounded often after July 2, 1776—the result, possibly, of long immersion in the ancient Romans, who had specialized in grand gestures for the greater good. Jane Calvert would have it that the larger factor was his understanding of the martyr's vocation, viewed "in the light of Quaker theologico-politics."[8] "What can be more evident," Dickinson asked a now-unknown correspondent in August 1776, "than that I have acted on Principle?"[9]

Yet, as generally happens in the course of human events, the sense of sudden rejection by onetime admirers, genuine or false, was bound to rankle. Where were they now, these "summer soldiers and sunshine patriots"—to borrow, with a certain irony, Tom

Paine's characterization? Replying to another letter from Thomson, Dickinson held up the ideal of death as a fitting close to a career of promoting "every measure that could possibly lead to Peace or prevent her Return from being barr'd up—after cheerfully & deliberately sacrificing my popularity, and all the Emoluments I might so certainly have derived from it to principles—after suffering all the Indignities that my Countrymen now bearing Rule are inclined if they could so plentifully . . . shower down upon my innocent Head."[10]

"My innocent Head" told the tale, probably. On grounds the most likely and proper, as it seemed to him, he had done what he could for his countries—both of them, America and Britain—intending all for the best. He had been repaid with uncomprehending stares, or worse. The "immense bustle" he had once wanted to make in the world was reduced for the moment to cacophony. He had failed. Or not succeeded. Whichever was the better way of putting the matter, here was the heart of the matter.

Thomson—"your sincere & affectionate friend," he characterized himself to Dickinson—felt obliged to put in a word for his friend's critics and detractors: "They did not desert you. You left them. Possibly they were wrong, in quickening their march and advancing to the goal with such rapid speed." How Thomson wished they had "waited a little for you. But sure I am when their fervor is abated they will do justice to your merit."[11] Events would prove him correct. There was after all much merit needing ministration—and energetic exercise for the general good.

It may in this context be useful to recall that not all rejected heroes bear with patience their new, lower estates in life. They sometimes decide to change sides. Dickinson's monumental loyalty to the cause of his new country sets him apart entirely from the Tories—the American-born loyalists who for a complex of reasons, many of them thoroughly admirable, could not let go of king and flag. Among their number was Dickinson's old Pennsylvania Assembly adversary, Joseph Galloway, who would die an exile in England, shorn of the wealth he might have retained had he thrown in with the patriots.[12]

Dickinson was too much the American for any such enterprise. The land and the people were his own, no matter how some might choose to assess his conduct. Accusations concerning his "timidity" or overscrupulousness might stain the historical record, but no detractor has left mention of Tory scents on Dickinson's wardrobe. He loved liberty too much to concede its protection to those who had proved disdainful of its obligations and requirements.

In a recent, provocative assessment of Dickinson's doings in the summer of 1776, Jane Calvert focuses on his Quaker origins, using the word *Quaker* to define a structure of thought rather than a religious creed. His way was to disagree without obstructing. "His priority," she writes, "was always the preservation of American liberties by the surest means. Dickinson's record, when situated in the context of his culture, reflects not hesitancy, indecisiveness, or pessimism, but unambiguous resolve in favor of peace, liberty, and unity—and caution lest these things be lost in the heat of passion."[13]

So much for "cool, cool, conservative men" and other myths of the founding years. The wonder of the founding grows larger as the resources—emotional and intellectual—of the Founders come into focus, more and more.

TWELVE

"WILLINGLY TO RESIGN MY LIFE"

AND SO THE LABORS of John Dickinson, construed in terms of patching up the quarrel between Britain and her aggrieved colonists, duly came to an end. The case, as jurists were wont to say, was closed. For one party or the other—Crown or colonies, it was impossible to say—a distinctly unhappy outcome lay ahead.

Whenever the advocate loses a case for which he has contended long and eloquently, vexation and perhaps just a touch of shame are likely to brush against him as he gathers up his papers and departs the courtroom. Dickinson partook of various emotions as the victory of the impatient and the rout of the prudent—the painfully prudent, many would have said—provoked general joy and celebration. Yet the matter was done, and Dickinson had declared for home and liberty. He was on America's side, irrevocably. A few years later, outlining as a member of Congress some considerations for a possible peace treaty, he would explain two rules he had laid down for himself "as a Trustee for my countrymen"—first, not to trim but rather to "avow" his particular viewpoints on policy;

second, "whenever the public Resolutions are taken, to regard them tho' opposite to my opinion as Sacred because they lead to public Measures in which the Common weal must be interested, and to join in supporting them as earnestly as if my voice had been given for them." Past rejections of his positions might rankle. They were to play no part in framing his actions as a firm friend of his new country.[1]

Dickinson demonstrated that friendship by taking up arms against the British almost immediately upon his disappearance from Congress the day of the great July 2 vote. The popular accounts of Dickinson's part in opposing the Declaration of Independence—*1776* and the *John Adams* series—do him the justice of acknowledging his military activity. The British were carrying the war to New York—ironically, the only colony formally uncommitted to independence, to the point of requiring its delegates at Philadelphia to abstain from voting on the matter at all. Not until July 9 would the colony's provincial congress reverse its previous instructions to the delegates and endorse the Declaration of Independence, thus aligning all thirteen colonies in the new order of things. Sir William Howe had disembarked ten thousand red coats on Staten Island the very day of the vote in Philadelphia. Ten days later arrived a British fleet commanded by Howe's nautical brother Admiral Lord Richard Howe. The Howes came to outrank the "whys" as factors bearing on American resistance.

For support of Washington's army, which had shifted from Boston to New York, Congress ordered Dickinson's militia battalion to Elizabethtown Point, in New Jersey, across the Arthur Kill from Staten Island: "Col. Dickinson will make the proper disposition for relieving the said Rifle Companies [stationed at several nearby ferries]." Which he did, with, insofar as we know, efficiency but apparently not much strategic profit. The battalion, according to historically tested wartime precedents, sat, and sat some more. On August 10 it mustered 531 men fit for duty, not counting 52 who had deserted, fallen sick, or gone on "furlow." Colonel Dickinson only four days earlier had complained to Pennsylvania's colonial government of unrest among the troops. The next day he reported two desertions, calling on the government "to discourage such Behaviour." On the twenty-third—as Howe was landing troops on Long Island—Dickinson learned that his battalion had been called home. The rowdy, radical new government then running Pennsylvania undermined his authority by putting its battalions in the charge of two brigadier generals elected by the soldiers.

By the end of September, Dickinson—a duck out of the political water in which he felt natural—was done with the military. He handed in his resignation, emphasizing his readiness for "service as a volunteer in the next call of the militia of the city and neighborhood." Horseman as he was, he had the faculty to know himself ill-suited for the military life, considered as a succession of marches, encampments, and battles. In August he had written to his friend Charles Thomson, "My books and my fields are intercourse and employment for which my constitution is better formed than for the toils of war."[2] No insignificant factor was the always shaky state of his health—especially his gout. Several years later he would tell Caesar Rodney, governor of Delaware (as well as a cancer sufferer), of how he had been "for Some time exceedingly indisposed."[3] His military experience cannot have kindled by much his appreciation of fire and sword as instruments more suited to the present cause than talks and time.

The telling point was that Dickinson willingly did what his state and country asked of him: the course of action fixed upon, the time for talking foreclosed. There was no more to say; there were horses to mount. Of his brief military endeavors Dickinson's nineteenth-century biographer, Charles J. Stillé, says, accurately, "He sacrificed not only his opinions but his pride to the true instinct of patriotism.... He was all the more anxious to do his duty, for the sentiment of devotion to his country seemed to absorb his whole life." A slightly defensive tribute but hard to contradict on the basis of exterior evidence.[4]

The example Dickinson set for others was striking even by the standards of the times. Just two members of Congress put themselves forward for military service. Thomas McKean of Delaware, a signer of the Declaration, was one. Dickinson, the noted nonsigner, was the other.[5]

He himself wrote to Charles Thomson in August: "As for myself, I can form no idea of a more noble fate than, . . . willingly to resign my life, . . . for the defence and happiness of those unkind countrymen whom I cannot forebear to esteem as fellow citizens amidst their fury against me." Duty, in his mind, subjugated resentments, however just he may have thought them.[6]

UNITING THE COLONIES

The Revolution, as of the summer of 1776, had passed in large degree into hands better skilled at a particular kind of minutiae—the military kind—than were John Dickinson's. Still, ample scope remained for the exercise of his own special gifts. He had lent those gifts already to the cause of uniting the colonies as an effective whole.

Immediate or postponed independence had been far from the only large question facing Congress in the early summer of 1776. There was additionally the issue of whether such geographically and culturally diverse colonies could pull together in the politi-

cal harness. The matter had scarcely arisen before, save when delegates from north and south and places in between sought a unified response to British affronts such as the Stamp Act. Dickinson
raised it memorably by questioning, in lonely fashion, on July 2,
the colonies' fitness to take on the British empire. Admonishing
the throne and the Parliament was weighty business, but hardly of
the same gravity as adjusting the power balance among the various
colonies, and also between what was local and what national in
scope and importance. The problem was not precisely terra incog-
nita, but it was certainly terra nova: more glimpsed than explored.
If there was now to be a change in central governments—from the
royal and remote to the popular and close at hand—delicacy in
footwork was the starting requirement.

Delicacy was hardly the word that came first to mind when
the attributes of the more forward-minded patriots—John Adams,
for instance—were taken into account. Adroit hands and minds
were essential to the task of preparing a governmental framework.
Whatever his skepticism as to the timing for independence, Dickinson was too consequential a figure not to be brought into the
project. "Men still welcomed his caution and legalism in this area,"
Garry Wills writes in *Inventing America.*[7]

During the recess provided for consideration of the Lee resolution on independence, Congress named a thirteen-man committee
to sort through the various notions afloat concerning governmental forms and then to devise a plausible structure. Some men of real
ability—McKean of Delaware, Edward Rutledge of South Carolina, and Roger Sherman of Connecticut, among them—sat on
the committee. Representing Massachusetts was Sam Adams. The
ablest of the lot in various ways was the Pennsylvania Farmer, who
quickly assumed a leadership role. "There is little doubt," writes
the historian Merrill Jensen, "that Dickinson was dominant in the

committee. His prestige as a writer and the honesty of his convictions led men to respect him whether they agreed with his political views or not."[8]

Central to the committee's work was the necessity of addressing the oldest of all human questions, its roots struck deep in the soil of Eden. The question was that of power and authority. Who, in any particular human arrangement, from family to nation, came first? Whose will and needs were to dominate whose? It was much more than an academic question in the summer of 1776. A variety of colonial establishments, soon to uproot themselves from the only political authority they had ever known, required a form of government that afforded unity and also important protections for their individuality and dignity. There was bound to be great thrashing about as the congressional draftsmen pulled this way and that. Dickinson's advantage over the other committee members was his experience of sorting out intellectually the basic power questions that had long embroiled mother country and colonies, of weighing competing claims in the light of experience, sidestepping what would come eventually to be called ideology. The relationships that Dickinson sought to compose were real ones, involving real people and real interests. A careful lawyer who was also a historian by temperament and avocation was sure to understand the intricacy of the task.

If the colonies were to succeed against the infinitely better prepared British, they needed unity over all things. Franklin's amusing maxim about the merits of "hanging together" rather than separately tracked Dickinson's own thinking. Indeed, a draft Franklin had essayed a year earlier for unified government provided Dickinson and the committee a starting point. To Dickinson, as to Franklin, the need for a strong central government was clear. Without such a government, how could the centrifugal tendencies of thirteen only tentatively related colonies be kept in check? There was in these reasonings something of British imperial theory. British statesmen, Pitt included, were inclined, in greater or lesser degree, to grant the colonies some latitude and freedom of action, but few if any disputed Britain's right to call the imperial tune or the necessity for playing such a tune.

The term *central government* today by no means connotes what it did then. The notion in 1776 was not to entangle thirteen colonies in a web of federal policies and regulations spun to define broadly acceptable modes of living. Rather, the idea was to maximize the colonies' capacity to face the unknowable in a manner conducive to the good of the great majority. Dickinson, as Jack Rakove writes, "envisioned a confederation whose own needs would enjoy clear precedence over the rights of the states."[9]

What is known as the Dickinson draft of the Articles of Confederation[10] gave the new "confederacy" a name: the United States of America. States distinct from one another yet nevertheless united was the meaning of the term. The colonies were "never to be divided by any Act whatever," according to Article II of the Dickinson draft. They were bound "to assist one another against all Force offered to or attacks made upon them or any of them."

Then notice Article III. Each colony was to "retain and enjoy as much of its present Laws, Rights and Customs" as it saw fit, as well as authority over "its internal police." But all this was "in matters that shall not interfere with the Articles of this Confederation." The good of the whole came before the preferences of the parts. Colonies could not, without congressional consent, enter into treaties with foreign powers (Article IV) or with one another (Article V); nor could they maintain their own standing armies (Article IX). Every colony (Article XII) was to abide "by the Determination of the United States assembled, concerning the Services performed and Losses or Expences incurred by every Colony for the common defence or general Welfare." Colonies were to recognize one another's boundaries and acquire no new Indian lands "before the Limits of the Colonies are ascertained" (Article XIV). Each colony, irrespective of size, would have one vote in the national legislature that was to meet at Philadelphia. The terms of peace and war were in the hands of the national government (Article XVIII). A Council of State—"one Delegate from each C[o]lony"—had what might be called executive authority over military and naval operations, the paying of national bills, and the shaping of proposals "for the Consideration of the United States" (Article XIX).

Given the assemblage of minds on duty in Philadelphia, most with powerful notions of their own, a practical advocate such as Dickinson could hardly have expected to have his way in all things. "He himself admitted," says Jensen, "that every article was bitterly fought over, and the existing evidence indicates that the disputes were long and sharp."[11] A Dickinson proposal ("the most innovative of the entire draft," says Rakove) that would have prevented additional state restrictions on religious exercise died at the committee level.[12] Nor would the committee entertain Dickinson's idea of forbidding states to lay tariffs on imports from other states. Larger colonies wanted voting power in the Congress proportionate to their populations, but Dickinson, representing the populous colony of Pennsylvania, prevailed on the point of equality.

The Dickinson draft, considered two centuries later, resembles in important respects a legal contract more than a national charter. Charter it certainly was not. It was too soon for that. Independence had first to be won. And so one of the chief impressions is of minute, lawyerly stipulations—for example, the colonies were to keep up "a due Number of Field Pieces"; "The United States assembled" would "make Requisitions from the Legislature of each Colony, or the Persons therein authorized by the Legislature to execute such Requisitions, for the Quota of each Colony," whereafter the legislature would appoint officers and train the men; the Assembly of the States would publish a journal of proceedings, with transcript available on request.[13] A large enterprise was in train. Everyone had to know what was expected: what were the rights in prospect, what were the limitations on rights.

To Edward Rutledge, the whole, slightly legalistic exercise was exasperating. With the debate on independence about to commence, he complained in a letter to John Jay of New York that the Dickinson plan "has the Vice of all his Productions to a considerable Degree"—"the Vice of Refining too much." Rutledge was no happier with the plan's bias in behalf of central authority. He saw "The Idea of destroying all Provincial Distinctions" as subjecting the colonies "to the Govt. of the Eastern Provinces." "I am resolved," he said, "to vest the Congress with no more power than is absolutely Necessary."[14]

An argument, a debate that would resound to the present day, had commenced. For the short run, the Congress would resolve it in behalf of the states. The parts, in immense degree, would prevail over the whole. Dickinson's sudden departure from Congress, and brief absorption into military affairs, left his draft of government—a draft not yet fully fleshed out—incapable of the advocacy he would have afforded it. A considerable irony of the crucial month, July 1776, is that the war Dickinson had sought to avoid took him from sight just when his political and philosophical touch was most needed. Had he remained in Congress to steer the Articles through to adoption, history might have passed more briskly over his defeat on the second of July. At a minimum, Congress might have adopted a document better adjusted to the needs of a unified resistance.

The final draft of the document Congress did adopt the following year was, as Jensen writes, "a pact between thirteen sovereign states which agreed to delegate certain powers for specific purpose, while they retained all powers not expressly delegated by them to the central government."[15] This change sprang in 1777 from the initiative of Thomas Burke of North Carolina in putting forth successfully a new Article II, which declared, "Each state retains its sovereignty, freedom, and independence . . ."[16] The central government as finally given shape in November 1777 lacked the power to tax, the power to regulate commerce among the states, and the means to compel obedience to its own enactments. Forrest McDonald has noted an additional irony: the states, so jealous of their taxing prerogative over that of the Crown, turned with zeal to exercise that prerogative. "The level of taxes during the 1780s," writes McDonald, "was ten to twenty times prewar norms, and the increase in the volume of legislation, despite ostensible constitutional checks on the legislative power, dwarfed the increase in taxes." That was not the end of it. "Legislation was enacted to regulate what people could produce and sell and what they could charge for it; to interfere systematically with private commercial transactions and suspend the obligations of private contracts; to prohibit the purchase of luxuries, prescribe what people could eat and drink, and govern what they could wear; to regulate private morality, indoctrinate the citizens with official dogmas, and suppress contrary opinions; to inflate the currency deliberately to pay for the ever-mounting costs of government."[17]

The garment Dickinson had woven with such care his successors turned inside out. A decade later, as the consequences of this reversal became clear, he would put his powers of prophecy and analysis again to work in behalf of reclaiming the original vision—the whole as more than the simple sum of its parts. McDonald has written, provocatively: "An interplay of state and local jeal-ousies resulted in the emasculation of the Articles. If Dickinson's articles had been adopted, the Constitution might never have been necessary."[18]

A NEW ORDER

A new spirit was abroad in the aftermath of July 1776, animating programs and provisions that wanted trying out if only because there had been no occasion previously to try them out. It was the case even in hidebound or, as the case might be, complacent Penn-sylvania, where John Adams's and the Congress's call for reorga-nization of colonial governments had resulted in the overthrow of the proprietors and the charter of 1701. The new common-wealth's large populations of working-class Germans and Scotch-Irish desired to put behind them a past associated with ideals and leaders no longer in fashion. A revolutionary rump convention of the old Assembly—proclaiming if not exactly proving its legal authority—met in July and named new delegates to Congress. Pointedly missing from the new slate was the name of the only member of the old slate to refuse adherence to the Declaration of Independence.

Of this occasion Dickinson would write: "I had not been ten days in camp at Elizabethtown, when I was by my persecutors turned out of Congress. While I was exposing my person to haz-ard, and lodging every night within half a mile of the enemy, the members of the Convention at Philadelphia, resting in quiet and safety ignominiously voted me, as unworthy of my seat, out of the National Senate."[19] Anger and hurt competed for dominance in the scale of Dickinson's emotions. He had spoken the truth as he knew it. The punishment had begun; nor did it look like stopping. He would have to ride it out. It stung, all the same.

Pennsylvania's new government did much more than dismiss the Pennsylvania Farmer from its congressional delegation. It drew up and promulgated a state constitution determinedly radical in some of its assumptions. Among these: the state needed no executive power—the authority of the Assembly would suffice; all males who paid a poll tax qualified to vote, provided they swore not to oppose the government. Forrest McDonald says the document established "what was little short of a totalitarian democracy. A tightly knit band of doctrinaire, uncompromising zealots . . . drew this power from and wielded it through the militia and the city mob."[20] The breathless events of the past few months had swept Pennsylvania toward destinations hardly thought of earlier, save perhaps by Tom Paine. A great sorting-out process had commenced. Old, new; wheat, chaff—it was all to be weighed and sifted. Events would determine which elements survived.

It would not have been characteristic of John Dickinson, howsoever chastened, to withhold his viewpoints and instincts from the fray. In the fall elections of 1776, leagued with friends and supporters who favored steadiness in the face of tempests, he stood for the Assembly and won, most voters in Philadelphia County (himself included, almost certainly) having decided to ignore the oath requirement. Hardly had he taken his seat before he urged the Assembly to call a convention that would revise—meaning from his own standpoint moderate and temper—the new constitution. The new order in Pennsylvania had no interest in opening doors to the return of anything old. Understanding how the land lay, Dickinson declined to sit any longer in a body he already viewed as illegal and improper. In December, with rumors and reports in the air concerning a British descent upon Philadelphia, he decamped with his family to the estate in Kent County, Delaware, where he had grown up.

The intimate connection between Pennsylvania and the former tributary counties that made up the new state worked to his own advantage, of course, but also to that of the large neighborhood privileged to call upon him for service. Delaware in 1776 had elected him—a little defiantly, in view of the doings up the Delaware River—to a seat in Congress. He besought his old friend George Read, then the governor, to dispense him from that obligation in view of, among other things, his ill health. Read agreed, but Delaware tried again, in January 1779. He accepted this time, taking his seat on April 23. He was warmly welcomed back, Stillé says, "by those who looked to him for aid and support in the arduous work which they had undertaken."[21] Who likely, as well, had better things to do than dredge up old resentments concerning once-valued allies.

Dickinson had not changed his views on constitutional theory. He wrote Caesar Rodney, the governor, the following month: "It may so happen in managing the Affairs of so extensive a Confederacy, that particular States may be more interested in certain points than the Confederacy in general....As a delegate I am bound to prefer the general Interest of the Confederation to the partial Interests of Constituent Members, how many so ever they be, & however respectable and meritorious."[22] He remained unafraid to stand by his beliefs. For all the defects the Articles of Confederation might have acquired since he deposited the original draft with Congress, he signed the document on May 5, along with Nicholas Van Dyke, making Delaware the twelfth state to accede to the new political order.

GHOSTS

There was still, of course, a war to be waged and won. Events pressed hard upon the colonies' richest and most strategically located city. British efforts to subdue Philadelphia commenced in August 1777. On September 11 Sir William Howe attacked Washington's position on the eastern side of Brandywine Creek, southwest of the city. Here Dickinson returned to military service—as a private serving in a force of Delawareans. As he recounted the matter several years later: "In the year 1777, . . . I became a private in captain Stephen Lewis's company; and in that capacity served with my musket upon my shoulder, during the whole tour of duty performed that summer by the militia of [Delaware], when the British army landed at the head of Elk, and was advancing toward [Philadelphia]. . . I served also in another manner—in riding from one place to another, to collect arms and ammunition."[23] It was a strange role perhaps for the author of the *Letters from a Farmer* to perform; but, then, the times demanded strange things of men and women in various stations of life. The battle went poorly for the Americans, who, after suffering twice as many casualties as the British, fell back toward Philadelphia. Whatever deeds Dickinson wrought at the Battle of Brandywine—his last reported engagement—McKean, governor of Delaware, plucked him that same month from the ranks, bestowing on him the epaulets of a brigadier general of militia. Promotion failed to keep at bay the various vexations that interfered with military service, chiefly lack of good health. He resigned his commission inside of a few months.

Meantime, Howe industriously cleared the Delaware Valley of colonial resistance, as far upriver as Philadelphia, and levered Washington and his army westward to Valley Forge. The city where Jefferson's Declaration was framed and proclaimed had lost its independence. British intentions now were supreme, as Dickinson and other patriots found to their cost. American raiding parties had made shows of defiance against the occupying army. The occupiers were having none of it. Orders went out for reprisals. In the neighborhood of the Germantown road, the British put the torch to seventeen American homes and estates. One was John Dickinson's beloved Fair Hill, with its gardens, prospects, and enviable library, where various delegates to the First Continental Congress—among them, John Adams—had enjoyed the city's hospitality. The next year, Howe and his red coats having moved on, a congressional delegate and Declaration signer from New Hampshire, Josiah Bartlett, surveyed the devastation. "The Country Northeast of the City for several Miles," he wrote, "is one common waste. The Houses burned, the Fruit Trees & others cut down & carried off, fences carried away, Gardens and Orchards destroyed, Mr. Dickinson & Morris's fine seats all Demolished."[24]

A few months earlier, writing to his wife, John Adams had trumpeted the accuracy of his prophecies concerning the "total neglect and disgrace" of "the Farmer"—who "turns out to be the man that I have seen him to be these two years."[25] It was not quite two years since the dinner at which Dickinson had welcomed Adams to Philadelphia and Fair Hill, impressing him with his "excellent Heart" and "ingenious" mind. The old days at Fair Hill were ghosts now—very like Fair Hill itself.

THIRTEEN

"THE SACRED VOICE OF MY COUNTRY"

WHATEVER THEIR FISCAL AND military shortcomings—which were plentiful—the colonists knew well the uses and challenges of government: a faculty not to be taken for granted, as we have learned in our own era from observing popular uprisings all over the globe. A rebellion must have headship and hierarchy, along with goals and organization, lest it topple like a house of cards. The need for leaders of character and understanding is never satiated in these circumstances. Which is to say, among other things, that John Dickinson's incorporation into the structure of colonial government had the aspect not only of good judgment but also of inevitability.

He had lost a particular (if urgent) argument. What of it? Only the loudest and most talkative when it comes to political differences were likely to doubt his patriotism. To Caesar Rodney of Delaware, Dickinson would write, in June 1779, at a moment of some discouragement for the colonial cause (the British having won important victories in the South): "Let us at this important

Crisis intensely recollect our duty to Heaven and our Country—
co-operate in our several stations with the Efforts of our Gallant
Brethren in the field."[1] As if patriotism were too small a commen-
dation for public service, there was the additional advantage of
Dickinson's large gifts as writer and counselor. It would have been
perverse, in other words, for the people of the middle colonies to
have shunned him as a leader.

Far from shunning him, they sought him out. Delaware, as
we have seen, wanted him as a delegate to Congress. He declined,
but the state persisted. At last, bearing Delaware's commission, he
returned in April 1779 to his familiar habitat, the State House in
Philadelphia. While there, he suffered a second punishment at the
hands of those whose connection with the colonies he had worked
to preserve. Lord Charles Cornwallis's surrender at Yorktown lay
only two months in the future when, in August 1781, a Loyalist
raiding party looted the Kent County estate to which Dickinson
had moved in late 1776. Returning to Delaware to deal with the
damage, he found himself drawn inadvertently into the state's politics. New Castle County wanted him, it transpired, as a member
of the Delaware governing council. He agreed—his first gingerly
step into a widening maw. Before the year was out, he was nomi-
nated as president—chief executive, that is—of the whole state.
The one legislative vote against his candidacy was his own, or so
historians surmise.[2]

John Dickinson was once more a public figure of consequence.
The gratitude he owed one of his two home states for its expression of confidence cannot have blotted out expectations of a return
someday to the other state, in whose affairs he had so long bus-
ied himself. Reaction to Pennsylvania's constitution of 1776—
generally described by historians as "radical"—had grown apace.
The radicals, mild enough by the standards of the sans-culottes

who were soon to emerge in France, with their guillotines and rigged tribunals, had subdued without formally depriving the large merchants and property owners. Among these, resentments and objections multiplied. For one thing, the 1776 constitution provided no effective checks on the unicameral legislature. Then there was the so-called test act, requiring of officeholders a vow never to alter the document responsible for that precise disability, in addition to others.

The radicals were distinguished by their predictable preference for paper money, the conservatives by their commitment to specie-backed currency, resistant to erosion in value on account of inflation. A debtor class perennially favors money whose value shrinks over time; a creditor class wants to be paid back in currency worth more or less the same as when the loan was made. By 1782 these fundamental differences in outlook had brought Pennsylvania politics to "the most heated state they had ever been in," declares the Dickinson scholar J. H. Powell. "Tempers of the people were hotly aroused, violence and threats of violence burst out in every county."[3] Pennsylvanians came gradually to recall the advantages of a government competent to maintain general prosperity, if in a setting not much more than quasi-democratic. Increasingly they wanted sound money and tax reforms that lightened the excessive burdens of freeholders. Public officials, by these lights, ought to be educated men of property, dwelling high above temptations to corruption, men of refinement and broad viewpoint—gentlemen, in short. Was there anyone who better fitted the template than John Dickinson?

Joseph Reed, who had been adjutant general of the Continental army and was no friend to Dickinson or his personal style, was stepping down after three one-year terms as president of the commonwealth. He cannot have been pleased to see the merchant class maneuvering to enfold Dickinson once again into Pennsylvania politics. This end the merchants achieved anyway by electing the president of Delaware to the Pennsylvania executive council in October 1781. "The day at last comes," Benjamin Rush wrote to Dickinson, "that will give freedom and happiness to Pennsylvania."[4] It was as much a sentimental effusion as an appraisal of Dickinson's ability to take up where he had left off years earlier in helping direct state policies and affairs. The new arrangement—a Delaware executive sitting in the councils of Pennsylvania—was decidedly odd: odder still after November, when this same Delaware chief executive accepted the presidency of Pennsylvania, having won a 41–32 executive council vote over the radicals' candidate, James Potter. The propriety of the arrangement consisted in reuniting in some spiritual sense neighboring territories that had functioned as one in the distant colonial past—while satisfying the perceived needs of the larger neighbor.

Delaware, which regarded President Dickinson as a great success—he had overseen the return to specie and the end of paper money—not illogically desired his full-time attention. After three months as chief executive of both states, he resigned his Delaware office, opting for Pennsylvania and the chance to repair what had been broken during his years of de facto exile.

MUTINY

It was in one sense an awful moment at which to recommence public service, given the tensions that had to be mastered; it was in many other senses an excellent moment. The Revolution had effectively ended with Cornwallis's surrender to George Washington. Even if the British maintained control of the seas and of most important

American ports, independence was a reality. There would be peace at last, and reconstruction. Decisive and imaginative leadership at the state level would repay people and leaders alike.

The Dickinson presidency of Pennsylvania, from the standpoint of the so-called Republicans who craved deliverance from radical exactions, is a paler affair than one might have expected under the circumstances. Nothing very dramatic occurred during Dickinson's three one-year terms in office—not even at the start. Writes the historian Robert L. Brunhouse: "Although the Republicans had control of the Assembly from 1782 to 1784, they effected no major changes in form or organization of the government." They spent their time instead reorganizing, regrouping.[5]

For one thing, neither of the two sides in the political saga had the voters' unobstructed ear. In 1784, so far from disappearing as a vital force after their defeat, the radicals actually regained control of the Assembly. It was for Dickinson, during his three-year presidency, to do the best he could, primarily by insisting on sound-money policies. Another accomplished Pennsylvanian, Robert Morris, who, like Dickinson, had absented himself from Congress's vote on independence (though he signed the Declaration in August), labored brilliantly to the same end. Morris had overseen colonial finances during the war. He was a sound-money man to his fingertips—eventually ruined in business life by overestimating his own credit.

In a career crowded with great moments amid great crises, Dickinson's postrevolutionary stewardship of Pennsylvania seems a slight episode. Powell rates the Dickinson presidency as lacking the touch the postrevolutionary moment seemed to require: his programs of economic progress and social and legal reform unremarkable, his attention insufficient to the task of building a political base.

A brilliant mind is notoriously not the same thing as a politically nimble mind, always on the lookout for openings and breakthroughs. Dickinson was neither reformer nor reactionary. More philosopher and prudent lawyer than anything else, he focused intently on the balance between order and liberty—anxious for freedom, anxious for the stability on which in the end freedom depends. He appears to have been most interested in legal questions. Nor, as Powell notes, did the Pennsylvania presidency confer much power anyway: "The executive was a plural one, the presidency a presiding office only.... He could never act except as one member of the Council, and on the most important issues...he could never carry with him even his own supporters in the Council."[6]

The event from those presidential years that has come down to us most vividly—military confrontations being inherently vivid—is the mutiny that occurred over how and when the national government would pay what it owed the soldiers it was starting to demobilize. It was not much of a mutiny as mutinies and spontaneous uprisings go: nothing like Shays's rebellion a few years later, when armed Massachusetts farmers demanded paper money and debt relief. In June 1783 one furloughed Pennsylvania regiment, doubtful of Congress's willingness to pay in a timely fashion, sent to the State House a demand for settlement. The secretary of war, General Benjamin Lincoln, an officer of courage and merit, managed to calm things down. A few days later, nonetheless, 250 to 300 soldiers took it into their heads to march on Congress to obtain their money. Surrounding the State House, they gave Congress the sharp jolt they had intended. Congress, not unreasonably under the circumstances, sought official protection.

Dickinson and the state council, much as they might deplore this access of mob rule, hesitated to call out the militia, fearing worse effects than would come from waiting out the mutineers for a couple of days. That was enough for Congress, which decamped for Princeton, New Jersey, not to return for seven years. Thereupon the mutineers' morale fell, and their leaders fled. Dickinson finally called out five hundred militiamen. This brought the mutineers around. They submitted to a lecture from Dickinson himself, and that was the end of the matter—except that the council's unwillingness to offer Congress protection had sent the country's government into exile from the place where the great national saga had commenced. Authority, furthermore, had forfeited the chance to make known that it would have no traffic with public disorder. A lesson that might have been put across for the benefit of a young and untested nation went untaught and unlearned.

VALERIUS

As it was, Dickinson had been having a rough introduction to the new school of Pennsylvania politics. The relative closeness of his election as president was a reminder that backers of the radical 1776 constitution had by no means undergone mass conversion to Dickinsonism. Not all Pennsylvanians wished the old grandees, Quaker and otherwise, restored to power. Some said so—with fury and virulence. A certain "Valerius"—whether or not named for the Valerius Publicola who had helped found the Roman Republic—aimed his sling at the forehead of John Dickinson and duly slung, in a series of four letters to the *Freeman's Journal*. No one knows the author's true identity. Possibly it was Joseph Reed, Dickinson's presidential predecessor, though the idea of so highly placed a figure stooping so quickly to anonymous abuse of his successor strikes a false note. Dickinson's niece, Mrs. Deborah Logan, identified a future secretary of war, John

Armstrong, as the villain of the piece. The irony here was that Armstrong had read law under Dickinson. Nothing but goodwill had passed between the two, so far as Mrs. Logan professed to know.[7]

James Wilson and a few other Dickinson allies were likewise the targets of anonymously delivered beatings and poundings. But Valerius's production—"brilliant and reckless," by Charles Stillé's accounting—raked every deck with hotshot, from bow to stern. Valerius scourged the new president of Pennsylvania for opposing the Declaration of Independence and the Pennsylvania constitution of 1776; for fleeing the enemy against whom he had encamped in New Jersey; and for depreciating the depreciated currency that passed among Americans in the last stages of the war. The man had "boundless ambition" and the gift of dissimulation: "He was the early and persevering enemy of the independence of America." His motives were awful, his techniques no less so. He himself was awful: an unreliable minister to the commonwealth's integrity and well-being.[8]

An odd side to an age of grace in manners and especially literature was the savagery into which eighteenth- and nineteenth-century political discourse could descend. There is a ferocity in the journalism of America's early national period that can take modern readers by surprise. From pseudonymous shadows spring ambushes meant clearly for purposes other than the uplift of thought and perception. One confesses, a little perversely, to finding a certain charm in some of these onslaughts, owing to an elegance hardly ever encountered on modern websites or in blogs. Take note, for instance, of the rapier lunge meant for the carcass of one leading Dickinson ally: "Could the human mind be dissected with the same skill as the body, it must puzzle the most profound anatomist to discover one single virtue or quality which would recommend

John Montgomery of Carlisle to a seat in Congress." For better or worse, no one writes this way anymore!

Dickinson, though well accustomed by then to abuse and political venom, might have been forgiven for falling into a towering rage at Valerius's assault on his dignity. In fact, he turned the occasion to advantage. The "Vindication" (as Stillé would call it) that he submitted to the *Freeman's Journal*—after calling on friends and supporters to stay their hands—was noble and firm at the same instant. Dickinson's boiling point, as opponents from Joseph Galloway to John Adams had come to know, was comparatively low. He could fall readily enough into self-righteous outrage and on occasion had done so. Not on the present occasion—not visibly. He steadied his voice, put on what could be taken for a small smile of patience in the face of insult. His fifteen-thousand-word reply exhibits superb command of both rhetoric and temper.[9]

One by one, Dickinson swatted away the charges. He had opposed "making the declaration of independence *at the time when it was made*." The "disposition of the great powers" toward the colonies was at the time unknown. "The terms of our confederacy" had not been roughed in, nor the boundaries of the states fixed. His anxieties had not been borne out. He spoke "as an honest man ought to do, yet, when a determination was made upon the question against my opinion, I received that determination as the sacred voice of my country.... From that moment, it became my determination, and I cheerfully contributed my endeavors for its perpetual establishment." It proved that "the national council was right. There is a light in that constellation, sufficient to direct the vessel freighted with the fortunes of America, through the tempestuous ocean, upon which she sails, safe in the wish'd for port—if the people will but be guided by it." It was a lovely passage, full of grace and cheer.

The 1776 constitution of Pennsylvania? Yes, he had opposed it as "unnecessarily expensive, and not well-calculated as it might have been, for permanently securing and advancing the happiness of the people." He could reasonably have added that a great number of Pennsylvanians had since joined the clamor for replacing that document. He alluded to Delaware's success at getting rid of paper money and founding its future on specie. Speaking of money, all he had done by way of disparaging colonial paper was advise his brother, Philemon, in a private letter that fell into public hands, against receiving paper for the payment of debts in a British-occupied quarter of New Jersey. The accusation against his military service in New Jersey was readily turned aside. He had done his best there and departed upon his government's orders.

There was in his reply something of what might savor of self-pity, as when he wrote of his military service: "VIRTUE! *Thou* art not but a name.—For thou wert my comforter in that severe season of private and public afflictions, when my country re-wounded a bleeding heart, frowned on my humbly-faithful love,—and spurned me into the dust."[10] It was a bit much—a pitch too high for the provocation that excited it. There was more such material, done up in fine literary style but deficient, now and then, in the grave dignity that graced his summation.

It was to Dickinson's advantage, as he must have realized at length if not at first, that the Valerius letters were in the end small beer—more water under the bridge than flood waters accumulating behind the dam. After some early floundering, he saw, perhaps, his assailant's own vulnerability, and that of his other critics. They showed remarkable smallness of spirit. He stretched out a hand:

Which would you chuse, gentlemen, that the power I have should be well used or ill used? The former, to be sure. Then help me. Be my associates—I ask, I entreat your aid—I invite you to give me your advice freely and fully. The best way to promote the interests of the republic, is to prevent my errors, not to arraign them when committed....I am sensible of my weakness, and shall be glad to avail myself of those abilities and those virtues, for preventing any disadvantage from it to you or my other fellow citizens. I ardently desire that we may live together, under the true principles of society, equal liberty and impartial justice, happy, and generously contributing to rendering each other happy.[11]

Dickinson had climbed at last to the top of Valerius's rubbish heap and there found some footing.

The answer he gave cannot have been the one for which Valerius—whoever he was—had yearned. It showed for one thing that adversity and disappointment had seasoned the self-confident prodigy who was John Dickinson of Philadelphia: toughening him internally but also imparting to him a wider wisdom and understanding. He was fifty years of age. He had written much, spoken much, endured much. There was much still to do.

FOURTEEN

"ACTING BEFORE THE WORLD"

THE GOVERNMENT THAT THE states had established—*patched together* might better describe the achievement—between 1777 and 1781 served immediate purposes. That is to say, it fixed the terms on which the states could work together to secure independence. The Articles of Confederation were as much a matter of temperament as of statecraft. They embodied aspirations, hopes, distrusts, jealousies, and anxieties that were, in varying proportions, common to humanity.

Accordingly, the "United States of America"—as the Articles solemnly titled the new nation—fell short of true unity again and again. It was inevitable, possibly, that the pains of wartime, cooperating with the well-known infirmities of human nature, kept attentions fixed on matters of financial gain and profit. There were disputes over commercial policies and state tariffs. States acted in accordance with their own notions of the public good. Pennsylvania, for instance, levied a discriminatory tariff on ships owned by nations without treaty ties to the United States. Rivers of state-issued paper currency flooded the land, undermining instruments of credit and producing bumper crops of inflation. Shays's so-called rebellion in the Massachusetts back country, in 1786–87, brought together hosts of rural folk aggrieved over taxes and debts. Whatever they supposed themselves to be doing by blocking the sitting of county courts and conducting military drills, the farmers terrified the state's governing class, who crushed their enterprise with volunteer troops. When it came to money, the central government functioned only insofar as states actually came across with the funds it requisitioned from them. By 1786 New Jersey had grown bold enough to reject the government's financial requisition.

Enough, in most human situations, turns quickly to enough. Worried leaders of thought and finance throughout the young nation had reached that condition by 1786—save for those who had reached it earlier. It was time to do something, as John Dickinson was hardly alone in believing. He, and numerous others, cared too much for liberty to see it turn to license, with the prospect of license leading to strife and confusion—the very attributes of the just-ended conflict with Britain. "I do not conceive we can exist long as a nation," George Washington wrote to John Jay that summer, "without having lodged somewhere a power, which will pervade the whole Union in as energetic a manner, as the authority of the State Governments extends over the Several States."[1]

From September 11 to September 14, 1786, a dozen prominent state leaders met in Annapolis, Maryland, for an interstate commercial convention, centered on ways and means of rationalizing some of the built-in irrationalities of the existing system. Dickinson, a participant in every important general gathering of the era, was there, of course. Indeed, fellow delegates quickly promoted him to chairman of the meeting.

The call had gone out to all thirteen states. Just nine accepted. (Curiously, the host state, Maryland, never responded.) The delegates of four states failed to turn up in time, some having foreseen perhaps a longer meeting than circumstances actually indicated. This left New York, New Jersey, Virginia, Pennsylvania, and Delaware to promote to all thirteen states their design for a convention that might mend the defects of the Articles government while strengthening the union for the long pull. The Annapolis meeting picked Philadelphia as the site for the convention and May of the following year as the time to begin. Delegates, it was hoped, would "take into consideration the situation of the United States, and . . . devise such further provisions as shall appear necessary to render the Constitution of the Federal Government adequate to the exigencies of the Union." The Annapolis report was read to Congress, then meeting in New York City. Congress approved the contents, stipulating that the convention should confine itself to "revising the Articles of Confederation."

In mid-May the delegates began making their way to Philadelphia. They knew by then, most of them, not only the way but also the destination—the State House, where everything consequential in American life seemed to happen. Naturally John Dickinson was on hand, a delegate this time from Delaware. State leaders acknowledged not only the credentials of their most famous and accomplished statesman but also the peculiar peril of the smaller states. None was in fact smaller than Delaware, with a mere sixty thousand inhabitants. Could the likes of Virginia and Pennsylvania be counted on to respect its claims to something like moral equality in the Union? George Read, also a delegate from Delaware, expressed in a letter to Dickinson his suspicion that the larger states would "probably combine to swallow up the smaller ones by addition, division, or impoverishment."[2]

As it happened, Dickinson's views were well suited both to the necessities of the state he represented and to the vision animating the convention as a whole. He understood the need for a stronger central government; he gave every appearance of understanding equally well the importance of the states themselves and of their particular, locally founded interests. He was anything but the man to stand by and watch the nation gobble up and digest its constituent parts. Early in the deliberations, he moved that a majority of states be empowered to request that the national legislature remove the national executive. Dickinson "had no idea"—by James Madison's paraphrase of his remarks—"of abolishing the State Governments as some gentlemen seemed inclined to do. This happiness of this Country in his opinion required considerable power to be left in the hands of the States." He saw "the division of the Country into distinct States" to be "a principal source of stability. This division ought therefore to be maintained and considerable power to be left with the States." Not "all power"—merely "considerable power."[3] That was the urgent point. The states were not to rule; neither were they to be ruled from some far-off federal Persepolis. Getting the balance right was going to require work—for which Dickinson was ready in spirit, whatever the challenges his health might pose.

For the opening day of the convention, May 14, only the delegates from Virginia and, as might be expected, the host state of Pennsylvania turned up. Not until the twenty-fifth was there a quorum. On the twenty-ninth, James Madison recorded in his copious notes on the convention proceedings that "John Dickinson and Elbridge Gerry, the former from Delaware, the latter from Mass.ts took their seats."[4] Dickinson was fifty-four years old—far from the convention's most ancient member, that distinction belonging to eighty-one-year-old Benjamin Franklin, who had to be transported to the State House in a sedan chair, such was the pain he endured from gout and stones. Ranked behind Franklin in chronology were Roger Sherman, sixty-six; William Livingston, sixty-three; George Mason, sixty-two; and George Wythe, sixty-one. The average age of delegates was forty-four.

Dickinson was, in the words of Charles Stillé, "one of the most active members of the Convention." There, predictably, he was a presence—more for qualities of mind and counsel than for style and personal magnetism. Plagued by poor health, as was so often the case, at the convention he had a frail, almost ghostly appearance. A delegate from Georgia, William Pierce, who had never heard him before, found him "an indifferent Speaker" due to "an affected air of wisdom." Even so, Pierce charitably pronounced him "a good writer" who would "ever be considered one of the most important characters in the United States." Memories of the earlier Philadelphia convention, in the summer of 1776, had lightened, so far as Dickinson's ideas and activities were concerned. There seemed no necessity of raking up the dead past: who thought and said what, and why, in the week of the famous vote for independence.[5]

A VISION FOR AMERICAN GOVERNMENT

It was all to be done, in accordance with...nothing, actually. Nothing that bound, nothing that adhered (as in England) to a thing that in turn adhered to another thing. The whole enterprise was fresh and therefore terrifying to a degree. As North Carolina's delegates observed in a communication to their governor, "An union of Sovereign States, preserving their civil liberties and connected together by such Tyes as to Preserve permanent & effective government is a system not described, it is a Circumstance that has not Occurred in the History of men."[6] The delegates to the Great Convention had it in their hands to build for the ages or for a fraught and special moment. Contrasting viewpoints naturally abounded.

Two plans emerged early for contemplation by the fifty-five delegates (of whom just thirty-nine would sign the convention's final handiwork). The so-called Virginia Plan, offered by Edmund Randolph, called for "a national government" with three supreme branches—legislative, executive, and judicial—and a "council of revision" empowered to overturn laws of both the national and state governments. States in the lower house of the legislature would be represented in proportion to population. The upper house would be chosen by vote of the lower, with no assurance that smaller states would enjoy representation there of any kind. This is appropriately called the "big-state approach" to national governance. The smaller states countered two weeks later with the so-called New Jersey Plan, advanced by the state's attorney general, William Paterson. The Delawares and New Hampshires and Rhode Islands would concede to Congress the power to raise revenue and regulate commerce, but only if each state was provided a single vote in a one-chamber assembly.

As for John Dickinson, son of Delaware, citizen of the United States, loyal servant to an informed and tender conscience, the least that can be said is that he had arrived at the State House at a critical moment. Dickinson's lawyerly mind held a clear vision of the kind of government—he knew, from professional experience, the details would require ironing out—that could be relied on to promote the urgent ends of virtue and liberty. He understood how a free people should look and act, and what principles should adorn them. What a great opportunity confronted Americans, he would muse, months later, urging ratification of the Constitution. And "what an infatuated, depraved people must Americans become, if, with such unequaled advantages, committed to their trust in a manner almost miraculous, they lose their liberty? . . . They have held, and now hold *the true balance* in their government. While they retain their enlightened spirit, they will continue to hold it; and *if they regard what they owe to others*, as well as what they owe to themselves, they will, most probably, continue to be happy."[7] Whatever scheme of government emerged from the convention had to comport with such realities.

On May 30 the convention got down to the urgent business at hand. Delegates resolved themselves into a Committee of the Whole for contemplation of the Virginia Plan. Dickinson was beginning already to lend his gravity and knowledge to the occasion. He knew the confederation to be "defective" and generally useless. Something stronger, more vital, was wanted. His busy pen scratched out a motion favorable to the idea of "a supreme Legislature Judiciary and Executive" for "securing the Liberty and promoting the Happiness of the People." The three-man executive he envisioned—one member each from the New England, middle, and southern states—would enjoy staggered terms of seven years. Against the single executive subsequently proposed under the New Jersey Plan, he would note "no instance of its being ever done with safety." Of similar mind were Roger Sherman, George Mason, and Benjamin Franklin.[8]

Dickinson understood from hard experience the impossibility of allowing states to insist on their own way at the expense of the national good. That was the fallacious theory underlying the Confederation. There was, nevertheless, an offsetting principle: to wit, the states were a necessity. "The division of the Country into distinct States," Madison recorded him as saying on June 2, was a main "source of stability," along with "the double branch of the Legislature." This division "ought therefore to be maintained, and considerable powers to be left with the States." We might otherwise read our country's fate "in the history of smaller ones."[9]

Baron de Montesquieu's spectacular treatise of 1748, *The Spirit of the Laws*, had fixed English as well as American minds on the beauty of separate, offsetting powers within government. Dickinson opened the way to thinking about Montesquieu's principles within an American context. What was on hand that could play the role the English barons had played in checking royal power? The states. Naturally. They existed. There was no occasion for calling them magically into existence. "Dickinson," says Forrest McDonald, a careful student of the Constitution's intellectual origins, "alone had perceived that the United States already had institutional substitutes in the form of the individual states—which, in a manner of speaking, were permanent and hereditary. He therefore proposed a mixed system, partly national and partly federal, in which one branch of Congress would 'be drawn immediately from the people' and the other would represent the states as states and be elected by the state legislatures for long terms."[10]

In "a discourse of some length," as Madison put it, Dickinson fleshed out his vision of government by complementarity. A limited monarchy was "*one* of the best Governments in the world," yet "out of the question" for America, owing to the "spirit of the times—the state of our affairs." Nor had the former colonies the means of supplying the "House of Nobles" that a constitutional monarchy would require. As for representation in the national legislature, the dispute between large states and small ones "must probably end in mutual concession." He hoped that "each State would retain an equal voice in at least one branch of the National Legislature, and supposed the sums paid within each state [in taxes] would form a better ratio for the other branch than either the number of inhabitants or the quantum of property."[11]

On June 7 Dickinson proposed that individual states appoint the chamber we know as the Senate. This was in order (as the Massachusetts delegate Rufus King recorded) that "the mind & body of the State as such shd. be represented in the national Legislature" by "men of first Talents," including the wealthy. By Madison's account, Dickinson hoped for a senatorial component of "the most distinguished characters, distinguished for their rank in life and their weight of property, and bearing as strong a likeness to the British House of Lords as possible." He was, moreover, for appointing a large number of these "characters"—two hundred at least. This would "increase their consequence & weight & by combining the families and wealth of the aristocracy, you establish a balance that will check the Democracy." With "Democracy" not yet the mud-god to which later ages would build shrines, the convention could understand Dickinson as implying that things such as getting the job done outranked raw nose counting.[12]

What of Dickinson's reference to the robed and ermined parliamentary chamber of the country with which America believed itself to have broken for all time? The British political connection might be sundered, but British models—prudential models to which the colonists had pointed from the time of the Stamp Act— were in many minds persuasive. As McDonald has noted, there was in the new nation "a lingering taste for monarchy," refreshed by observation of the disorder into which affairs had widely fallen since severance of the royal connection. Dickinson, as we see, had remarked the value of limited monarchy, impractical as such an institution might be for America. Alexander Hamilton, for his part, desired a king-like, nonhereditary executive who would serve for life unless impeached—an element in the larger Hamiltonian hope to "go as far in order to obtain stability and permanency, as republican principles will admit."[13]

Madison thought the number of potential senators too large. He invoked the example of the Roman tribunes, who he said weakened in influence as their numbers increased. Dickinson came back: "Safety may flow from the variety of Interests," as under the British constitution. He spoke now for the states, drawing an inspired and helpful word image of the relationship he envisioned between states and the national government: "We cannot abolish the States and consolidate them into one Government. Indeed if we could I should be against it. Let our Government be like that of the solar System; let the General Government be the Sun and the States the Planets repelled yet attracted, and the whole moving regularly and harmoniously in their respective Orbits." He then swatted down Madison's contention as to the tribunes. There had been ten of them at most. Did anyone think the U.S. Senate should be so small? Bits of historical and astronomical information were coming together in a way that would astonish political eavesdroppers of later times.[14]

James Wilson, Dickinson's old ally and a strong nationalist, rose in dissent: "If the State Legislatures appoint the Senate, the principle, which has formerly operated the ruin of antient Confederacies, will be received and cherished, in that we are about to establish." He desired that the people themselves elect the Senate. A vote was called for. Wilson's proposal failed, whereupon the convention unanimously backed Dickinson's motion that state legislatures elect the Senate.[15] The Dickinson plan gave way in the early twentieth century to direct popular election, on the insistence of the progressive movement, which saw indirect election as defiled by the power of railroad and mining magnates. The country had come around to Wilson's perspective, without necessarily recalling its origin. That by no means disproved the value of the old formula, which reinforced the partnership forming between states and national government for the efficient running of the country. Planets and sun were working together, as originally projected.

Dickinson's overall vision for an American government he had reduced to writing by mid-June. Though he seems never to have introduced a "Dickinson Plan" as such, still he argued during the long summer for the specific elements that revolved in his mind, and against proposals he found wrong or unlikely. Of particular interest to him was the concept of staggered terms for members of both houses of Congress—an idea "borrowed from the antient Usage of England," as Madison noted down his words. "He supposed biennial would be inconvenient. He preferred triennial . . . by an annual election of one third." As to who might be entitled to vote, Dickinson could not speak warmly enough of the country's freeholders. "We are safe," he said, "by trusting the owners of the soil—the Owners of the Country." They were "the best guardians of liberty," as over against "the dangerous influence of those multitudes without property & without principle." There was no silk-stockinged snobbery in such an affirmation. "He doubted the policy of interweaving into a Republican constitution a veneration for wealth. He had always understood that a veneration for poverty & virtue, were the objects of republican encouragement." Gouverneur Morris—an aristocrat by taste and breeding, possibly the last American anyone would mistake for a Tom Paine acolyte—saw property qualification as protection *against* aristocracy. He supposed that nine-tenths of Americans were freeholders.[16]

A SENSE OF DUTY

While the Constitution of the United States was in preparation, Dickinson's physical constitution evidently fell into disrepair. A family member, Mary Norris, on July 4 reported "Cousin Dickinson" as faring "very poorly" under the stresses of the convention, in consequence requiring "Rest & quiet." For more than a month, from late June to late July, there is no record of his having spoken on the floor. Whether or not he was present on specific occasions during this period, the daily notes of the convention make no mention of him. Silence on important occasions was not reckoned as a Dickinson hallmark. Nor was inattention to ongoing affairs. Doubtless the Delaware delegation—and other friends, just as likely—kept him constantly informed.

Despite his various infirmities, Dickinson's sense of duty drove him hard. Notes of speeches he prepared during the period speak of a Dickinson vitally engaged by the proceedings, perpetually hoping to reinsert himself into their midst at the earliest opportunity. He had useful things to say, as in a speech prepared for the second week of July, when the convention was debating westward expansion. He asseverated on the prospect of new states' arising, requiring inclusion in the Union. "Is each new state," he asked, "instantly to start into an Equality of power by its Numbers only. The Inhabitants will undoubtedly be very numerous but poor in Comparison with the others." Pennsylvania had had some disagreeable experience of the poorer portions' disposing of "the whole Property of the State." He concluded, "Every new state [should] be put on the same footing with the smallest."[17]

In notes for another speech, Dickinson took up for the smaller states, such as his own. They posed no danger. "Their condition teaches them political Virtues and suppresses political Vices." He spoke a word for the patriotic attributes of his own state: "Thro the little State of Delaware, the Army of the Enemy passed, while her whole seaboard was exposed to the continual Hostilities of her naval forces.... Weak as her arm was yet did her Mind ever waver?

No."[18] No other delegate can have understood so impartially, and perhaps so perspicuously, the large state–small state imbroglio. He had lived in both sizes of state; he had represented both sizes.

Debates involving how to apportion representation inevitably touched on the issue of slavery. Dickinson recognized the practical concerns, noting in a speech in August that unless the convention limited "the number of representatives to be allowed to the large States...the small States would be reduced to entire insignificancy, and encouragement given to the importation of slaves." Dickinson, however, did not stop at such political concerns. He was one of the few at the Constitutional Convention to express principled opposition to slavery.

Dickinson had himself been a slave owner, holding as many as three dozen slaves at one point. He was far from unusual in this respect among the delegates in Philadelphia. He was, however, unique in that he was the only one to have already freed his slaves. Here the Quaker influence seems to have shaped his views. Quakers had practiced slavery of a relatively mild form—the slaves themselves being chiefly house servants, bakers, bricklayers, carpenters, and the like—until awakened by the same moral-religious spirit that William Wilberforce later brought to the successful campaign against the slave trade in England. With antislavery sentiment growing more intense in Quaker circles, Dickinson manumitted his slaves, conditionally, in 1777, and by 1786 he had freed them all unconditionally. As early as 1776, in *An Essay of a Frame of Government for Pennsylvania*, he had proposed a law by which "no person hereafter coming into, or born in this country," would "be held in Slavery under any pretense whatever." In 1786, a year before going to the Constitutional Convention, he had written abolition legislation for Delaware, though the bill failed to pass. Dickinson came (as he later put it in a letter) to see slavery as "deeply, deeply injurious to the morals of the masters and their families."[19]

These strenuous views on the subject came through clearly in the arguments he prepared for the Constitutional Convention. The draft of the Constitution that the Committee of Detail submitted on August 6 stated that Congress could neither prohibit the slave trade nor lay any taxes on "the migration or importation of such persons." The measure, as Dickinson saw things, was too feeble by half. The day after arguing against the importation of slaves on the grounds that it would hurt smaller states, Dickinson took to the floor to challenge the slave trade directly. As Madison recorded it, the Pennsylvania Farmer declared that it would be "inadmissible on every principle of honor & Safety that the importation of slaves should be authorised to the States by the Constitution." His impassioned plea appears to have won him a seat on the Committee on Slave Trade, charged with working out a compromise. The committee proposed allowing Congress to regulate the slave trade beginning in 1800; the convention eventually accepted the compromise but pushed the date out to 1808.

Dickinson's struggles with ill health rendered him silent during the period when the "three-fifths" compromise was thrashed out. We need not speculate, even so, as to where he stood on the matter. By the terms of this much-mocked, internally inconsistent bargain, three-fifths of the slave population would be counted both for a state's representation in the lower house of Congress and for its apportioned direct-tax liability. In a speech he prepared in July (but was unable to deliver), Dickinson reminded his fellow delegates that they were "acting before the World." "What," he asked, "will be said of this new principle of founding a Right to govern Freemen on a power derived from Slaves"—those "incapable of governing yet giving to others what they have not"?[20]

The artfulness of the three-fifths compromise betokened nothing good in terms of the slavery question's divisive power. Yet as Dickinson recognized, the delegates wished to get on with their task. If logical inconsistency was the price of forward movement, the political world provided ample precedents. "The omitting of the *Word*," he recorded prophetically—that word being *slavery*—"will be regarded as an Endeavour to conceal a principle of which we are ashamed."[21]

"FOR ETERNITY"

By September, all was done. Like all the rest, Dickinson failed to get his way in all things. It was the nature of the great proceeding in which all were engaged. The document at hand was of greater weight in certain particular senses than any proclamation, however stirring, of the right to walk a different national path. John Dickinson had held aloof from the Declaration of Independence. He wished his name firmly affixed to the plan of government he had helped to shape, against physical odds.

It was not a matter merely of stepping up to a table and signing. Dickinson was spent. He longed to be home in the Wilmington town house where he had lived since laying down the Pennsylvania presidency. He wrote a letter asking his friend and fellow delegate George Read to sign for him. He sent along a "Bank bill" as his contribution for an "Entertainment" delegates were giving the "Gentlemen of the Town, from whom we have received Civilities."[22]

On September 17, along with his own name Read inscribed that of John Dickinson, integrating both forever with the vision of governance and freedom, freedom and governance, that had overlain the Pennsylvania State House in the summer of 1787.

At the previous State House signing, in July 1776, Dickinson had stood out by his visible absence. Four delegates who opposed the Constitution were absent from the signing, their names uncaricatured by history. They were Luther Martin and John Francis Mercer of Maryland and Robert Yates and John Lansing Jr. of New York. Nine who favored the Constitution, or said they did, neglected also to sign. Life was less feverish, less enpurpled, by this time. A humble act of conscience was no longer a matter for public judgment and inquisition.

It was with high sense of the occasion that Dickinson had spelled out in June his expectations. "We are not forming plans for a Day Month Year or Age, but for Eternity," he wrote. "Let us endeavour with united Councils to establish a Government that not only may render our Nation great respectable free and happy but also VIRTUOUS. Let us try to combine political Establishments with moral Virtue that if possible the first may be equal with the Duration of this World and an aid or at least not a Hindrance to the Enjoyment of another."[23] His heart had labored as tirelessly as his head.

FIFTEEN

"EXPERIENCE MUST BE OUR ONLY GUIDE"

JOHN DICKINSON'S DELAWARE, ON December 7, 1787, became the first state in the Union to ratify the new Constitution. Five days later, John Dickinson's—it seems not unreasonable so to describe it—Pennsylvania followed suit and six days after that New Jersey. There were eight more votes of approval in 1788 and one, North Carolina's, in November 1789. With Rhode Island's accession in May 1790, the Union, as contemplated at the great convention of 1787, achieved perfection.

The summer affair in Philadelphia might have exhausted many of its participants. That was certainly the effect on the Pennsylvania Farmer, a veteran by this time of two decades and more in the struggle for liberty. The struggle would go on—if, indeed, there was evidence to indicate such a contest ever would or could cease.

Dickinson had left the convention full of hope concerning the delegates' handiwork. If the document seemed imperfect, how did that render it different from every other human device? There was a certain principled clamor against it by the men history would call the Anti-Federalists, fearful as they were of a tendency they saw in the Constitution to ride down the states and exalt the national government. A nationalizing program had certainly been afoot at the convention. Dickinson saw the program as constrained in its essentials, or he would scarcely have allowed his name to appear on the final product. He would have battled it with the intensity of George Clinton and Robert Yates. Instead, he argued for ratification in a series of nine letters published in a Delaware newspaper in 1788. This was due, said an editor's introductory note, to "an alarming hesitation of some States to ratify the Constitution proposed by the Federal Convention in 1787."[1]

The *Letters of Fabius* are of a cast very different from that of *The Federalist Papers* of "Publius." Speaking broadly—very broadly— the study of Alexander Hamilton, James Madison, and John Jay was to explain the Constitution to the American people and hence procure its approval. What, after all, *had* been going on at the State House, behind closed doors, all those months as the nation wondered and fidgeted? Some explanation was clearly indicated—"the utility of the Union," the necessity of an "energetic government," the document's "conformity . . . to the true principles of republican government."[2] There was some of this in the Fabius letters, albeit painted with a broader brush. Dickinson had a large vision of the principles that animated a free people. To Fabius there was no good in examining "The Constitution of the Senate in Relation to Its Capacity as a Court for the Trial of Impeachment" (Hamilton's *Federalist* No. 65). Dickinson had other objects in mind.

For instance, the necessity of leaning upon "experience" for enlightenment and understanding. On the convention floor, Monday, August 13, Dickinson delivered (via Madison's transcription) his famous judgment: "Experience must be our only guide. Reason may mislead us." This was by way of arguing that money bills should originate with "the immediate representatives of the people." Such was England's experience. "Whence the effect may have proceeded he could not say; whether from the respect with which this privilege inspired the other branches of Govt. to the H. of Commons, or from the turn of thinking it gave the people at large with respect to their rights, but the effect was visible could not be doubted. Shall we oppose to this long experience, the short experience of 11 years which we had ourselves on this subject?"[3]

The conversation broadened once the Fabius letters came to be written. Dickinson extolled "the judgement of the most enlightened among mankind, confirmed by multiplied experiments,"[4] and applied to present circumstances. The Achaean League of Greek city-states, though imperfect, had successfully promoted "the true spirit of republicanism" through "the popular representation of each part, and the close combination of all"—an adumbration of the Constitutional Convention's approach to the subject. By contrast, the states of the amphictyonic council of ancient Greece had prospered only insofar as the various states "continued faithful to the union." When envies and emulations beset them, "they all sunk together, the envied and the envying."[5] A classicist by avocation and conviction, Dickinson liked harking back to the Greeks and Romans for precedents and admonitions. So did enough other classically trained Founders to give his invocations added resonance.

Balance—"an animated moderation"[6]—was the vital ingredient in the constitutional recipe. A true federation of states, and of interests, was under construction. As provided by the proposed Constitution, "the government of each state is, and is to be, sovereign and supreme in all matters that relate to the whole; and it will be their own fault if the several states suffer the federal sovereignty to interfere in things of their respective jurisdictions."

Union without domination beckoned to the states. The diversified representation in the three branches of government under the Constitution was "essentially necessary to the good government of an extensive republican empire." The convention had attempted "the best means of preservation. This is all men can do, and they ought to do. Will it be said, that any kind of disunion, or a connection tending to it, is preferable to a firm union?"[7]

And what was the constitutional project all about to begin with? Not control or even efficiency in execution but mutual aims and protection—the extinction of fears and the birth of mental tranquility, "or, in other words, that perfect liberty better described in the Holy Scriptures, than anywhere else, in these expressions— 'When every man shall sit under his vine, and under his fig-tree, and *none shall make him afraid*.' "[8] The purposes of God, joined to the aspirations of man—here was a vision worth fighting a revolution to achieve.

To the society for which God had designed man, freedom and security were fundamental. Thus the constitutional project: "Can any government be devised, that will be more suited to citizens, who wish for equal freedom and common prosperity, better calculated for preventing corruption of manners; for advancing the improvements that endear or adorn life; or that can be more conformed to the understandings, to the very nature of *man*," whose natural rights were "the foundation of his civil rights"?[9]

The document at hand might be construed as a blessing. It gave "the will of the people a decisive influence over the whole, and over all the parts." This "plain-dealing work," which eschewed complications, diffused "the blessings of equal liberty and common prosperity over myriads of the human race." In our desire to spread happiness among fellow creatures could be perceived the divine design.[10]

There was indeed much of divinity in the life that Dickinson commended to his fellow Americans, much of reverence, much of gratitude. The constitutional plan was not geared to domination, expansion, or world mission. The newborn America could—would—should—aim at the good life.

Such things were not at all the things to which Publius had drawn attention in the prodigious *Federalist Papers*, one of the world's greatest treatises on political science. *Federalist*, with its immense attention to detail, and its emphasis on the workings-out of a "separation of powers" doctrine not even mentioned in the constitutional text, complements the letters, and vice versa. Nodding his head to many of Publius's affirmations, Fabius raises his eyes, looks around him, and sees a new world unfolding. Dickinson's small production—a mere tail to the *Federalist* wolfhound, as most scholars seem to account it—never has received the attention it deserves merely on account of its distinguished author's originality. When published, nonetheless, the Fabius letters were appreciatively received: not least by George Washington, who wrote from Mount Vernon to a friend, April 27, 1788: "The writer of the pieces signed *Fabius*, whoever he is, appears to be master of his subject; he treats it with dignity, and at the same time expresses himself in such a manner to render it intelligible to every capacity."[11]

"The Constitution described by *The Letters of Fabius*," says Gregory Ahern of the Center for Constitutional Studies, ". . . is a model of prudence and moderation, based not primarily on theoretical arguments, but on experience and extensive knowledge of history"—that is to say, the hallmarks of Dickinson's thought.[12] The path to which the letters pointed was well defined, revealing at every turn views of the various ways humans behave both under stress and at rest. Dickinson's understanding of human nature was an essentially religious one: the product of long meditation concerning God's purposes and expectations for the descendants of those he bid, near the beginning, "be fruitful and multiply." Dickinson never ceased as a Quaker, or as one who sometimes received the ministrations of the Episcopal Church, or for that matter just as a Christian believer and close student of the Scriptures, to contemplate the ways of God toward men and, correspondingly, the obligations of men toward God. Whenever he looked around his countrymen's new work in the new world, he stole a backward glance. And an upward one.

Dickinson's view of the Constitution, Ahern submits, was that of "a moderate Federalist"—in other words, a man who understood the arguments both for a sufficiently strong national government and for the states as repositories of rights and bulwarks of protection for those same rights.[13] No man who had closely read accounts of Roman history had ever gone wrong by inferring from those accounts the propensity of ambitious men to license themselves as reformers—to the applause of the multitudes, to the enrichment of their favorites. (*What means this shouting? I do fear, the people choose Caesar for their king.*) Centuries had gone by. Many, too many, still loved a king—of whatever kind was nearest the lover's heart. As John Dickinson had written in the persona of Fabius: "History sacred and profane tells us that, *corruption of manners sinks nations into slavery*."[14] "*Soundness of sense and honesty of heart*" were the great expedients of the race. What was required was continual attention to their vitality. Easy was the descent to hell.

FABIUS RETURNS

Dickinson would never again sit in a great council of the republic (though he sat, formally, as a member of the convention that wrote Delaware's 1792 constitution, occupying for that year only an at-large seat in the state senate from New Castle County). He swept away invitations in 1788, endorsed by his friend Dr. Benjamin Rush, to represent Delaware in the new U.S. Senate. "I believe there is not a man upon earth besides myself," he wrote to Rush, "who can form any idea of the distresses, from weakness of body, that I have undergone by endeavoring to sustain a public character with some decency while laboring under such infirmities."[15] For the Pennsylvania Farmer, a man by no means ripe, at age fifty-five, for the sexton's shovel, a life of public service had crested. The contributions a Senator John Dickinson might have made to the plotting of America's national course are matters solely for speculation. He would have lent authority and deep wisdom to the proceedings: so much seems clear.

The affairs of the new republic became, to say the least, complex following ratification of the Constitution and the commencement of the first presidential administration, under George Washington, accomplished at Federal Hall, New York City, April 30, 1789. The greatest, most ingenious of machines, once prepared, is subject to obstructions and eventualities impossible to have foreseen with perfect accuracy. So with the United States, whose first, Federalist, administration undertook policies that broke, inevitably, the spirit of unity that prevails at the start of every great undertaking. The words and structure of the Constitution presupposed balance, but words, which connote different things to different people, give way to deeds. The ingenuity and vision of Washington's treasury secretary, Alexander Hamilton, in seeking to make good the country's credit by giving government bonds to the varied holders of American debt, advanced a notion of federal power larger than many could abide. Two rival theories as to federal power took shape: that of Hamilton, who saw the national government as keeper of order and promoter of prosperity; that of the Virginians, Jefferson and James Madison, to whom individual freedom was the larger necessity. The Federalists sat lightly to claims that the Constitution restricted this sort of government intervention or that one. The Republicans, as their opponents came to be known, took seriously those restrictions as protective of the citizenry in the face of government oppression. From the perspective of the early twenty-first century, the terrain of the late eighteenth century has the look of home: the same anxieties and urgencies, in large degree; many arguments the same, having to do with legitimacy and lawfulness and the purposes for which the nation's government was designed.

As one of the designers, John Dickinson, semiretired in Delaware, naturally took a keen interest in developments, though in a more detached way. A younger generation, generally speaking, was taking command of affairs. At a time when the unfledged Alexander Hamilton could not have distinguished between Blackstone and a leather fire bucket, Dickinson was commencing law practice in the colonies' most sophisticated city. James Madison was only slightly older than Hamilton. A decade separated Jefferson and Dickinson. As national affairs moved forward in the 1790s, Dickinson scarcely spoke up, his health perhaps inadequate to the task, his mind entitled to reckon up services rendered already rather than fix on new ones. "Exactly what part Mr. Dickinson took in [discussions]," says Charles J. Stillé, "it is not easy to say with certainty."[16] The principal point worthy of note is that of a growing attachment to the person and ideals of Thomas Jefferson: two farmers, as it were, leagued closer and closer in support of a strict understanding of those things the government could legitimately claim title to do and those it could not. Stillé calls Dickinson "the opponent of any measure which looked towards the centralization of the national power."[17] So it was with Jefferson, who dreaded the consequences of drawing "all government, domestic and foreign, in little as in great things . . . to Washington as the center of all power."[18]

Along with his fellow farmer—indeed, with most Americans—Dickinson walked purposefully into the camp of the French revolutionaries who startled the world on July 14, 1789, by storming the Bastille prison and initiating the social and political upheaval whose consequences still resound everywhere. In the events that ensued, Americans tended to find affirmation of their own forceful response to tyranny. Had not America in some material sense shown France the way? As Lord Acton was to observe, years later, "The ideas which captured and convulsed the French people were mostly ready-made for them"—by Americans.[19]

The executions of the king and queen and the onset of the Terror precipitated second, not to mention third and fourth, thoughts. Cleavages opened between Federalists and Republicans—Federalists denouncing barbarities that the revolutionaries perpetrated, Republicans open to viewing the new course of French history as beneficial in the main to the cause of freedom. Washington, on Jefferson's prompting, recognized France's new government while declaring neutrality as that nation fought off foreign adversaries, the British included. By 1798 reckless French behavior toward the United States had pushed the two countries into an undeclared naval war and the United States into military cooperation with the British.

A puzzlement of Dickinson's career, at least on the surface, concerns his fervent embrace of the French cause, especially in a second series of Fabius letters, published in 1797 and 1798. The French by most accounts had made a hash of things, unable to restrain passions and hatreds from below. The tumbrils rolled, and Madame Defarge's celebrated knitting needles clicked incessantly.

Arrayed against France's revolutionary armies on the battlefield were, among others, the heirs of the Great Charter and the Petition of Right, the beneficiaries of carefully derived protections for the rights of accused persons. The latter point had, or should have had, extra poignancy against the backdrop of French enthusiasm for beheading any suspected enemy of the people. Edmund Burke, who had been at one with Dickinson in the matter of the American colonists' rights against the Crown, had in his *Remarks on the Policy of the Allies with Respect to France* inveighed against the "atheistic and murderous barbarians" who had supplanted Louis XVI. These, he said, had dispossessed the owners of "the moral France." "The master of the house is expelled, and the robbers are in possession," Burke had written—with considerable evidence for such a broad claim.[20]

Suddenly the two prophets stepped apart from each other. Burke, for one thing, was speaking from within the moral and geographical compass of a monarchy such as the French had overthrown. He sniffed peril. Dickinson was speaking from outside—as the citizen of a republic, and much he preferred it that way. There was additionally, no doubt, the factor of geographical propinquity, or lack of it. A mere four miles of water, at the English Channel's narrowest point, separated revolutionary France from the England of maypoles and ancient loyalties. To England, in great and growing numbers, poured French refugees bearing tales of horror and death. Burke feared from the conflict in France explosions that would scatter French principles all over Europe, like droplets of plague. From the other side of the broad Atlantic, the view was necessarily more placid, the level of emotions lower.

Dickinson's defense of France's republican constitution owed its immediate origins to American policy toward France. A familiar, if now much more rotund and stately, presence surged into view— that of John Adams. It was not that Adams, the new president, wished war against the French. He did not; war was the Hamiltonian policy. At the same time, Adams could hardly look with indifference on France's attempts to bully the United States into collaboration with its purposes. A heavy-handed French attempt to extract a loan and a bribe from American peace commissioners recoiled on the perpetrators. The United States abandoned its posture of neutrality in the revolutionary struggle and authorized the seizure of armed French ships on the high seas.

The American Republicans, including Dickinson, were unready for such a riposte. They continued to see France, whatever its current behavior, as a much likelier ally for the United States than monarchical Britain. They wished not to write off a friendship that had been essential to achieving American independence. "She is fighting for us as well as for herself," insisted Fabius, "and we shall be safe too, if we 'Know the things that belong unto our peace,' and 'ensue' them." He continued: "If *France* should not succeed in the present contest, there is not an elective republic on earth that would not be immediately annihilated. Ours would be crushed at once—not under a limited monarchy, such as we abrogated twenty years ago as intolerable, but a *despotism*, for the question *now trying by combat*, is—between *Republicanism* on one side, and *despotism* on the other.... The dagger of assassination is at the breast of *America*; and *France* alone holds back the hand that otherwise would strike it in—*up to the hilt*." War with France was unthinkable under these circumstances: "If France can be slyly irritated into a declaration of war against us, or if we can be artfully wrought up to a proper degree of madness, and follow into a war those guides [Hamilton and his friends] who have long since lost their way, their point is gained."[21]

Dickinson was far from justifying the executions of Louis XVI—"one of the best of kings, probably of men," he called him—and of Marie Antoinette. He regretted "the reign of tyrants, or rather of monsters" that had followed—the Dantons, the Robespierres. The essential point was that France, then governed under a bicameral legislature and a five-man Directory chosen from its leadership, was "a REPUBLIC . . . and in that attitude standing upon her trophies, stretched out her right hand to us, and proffered us her friendship." Which friendship America would do well to accept.[22]

The rhetoric was too rich. The Directors were unimpressive men, by and large, and the revolution had unsettled much that for decade upon decade would await resettling. In the background lurked Napoleon Bonaparte, with his extraordinary abilities and smoldering ambitions. Who the "despots" were, standing ready to do in the United States, Dickinson left unclear. Only two countries could aspire to that distinction—Spain, which was pitifully weak, and Britain, which was indisposed to resume management of colonies that had proved a handful in the past.

Dickinson's case for friendship with the French was partly grounded in gratitude for their past assistance to the colonies— "Frenchmen fought, bled, and died for us," the Farmer reminded his readers—but one may suspect also an unconscious aversion to those Americans who felt an aversion to the French: the high Federalists, with their anti-Republican policies and their eagerness for the fellowship of the old mother country, Britain.[23] The Federalists, after all, felt little disposition to restrict the exercise of government powers not spelled out precisely in the Constitution. They could be viewed as dangerous, and so could their choice of friendships. John Dickinson was never of their kidney.

The second set of Fabius letters lacks the grandeur of the first, both as to aims and to enduring relevance. The second set offers at least a way of better understanding how the risks and opportunities of the republican vision were appraised by that vision's best friends: among whom, as always, John Dickinson was conspicuous.

FRIENDS AND FOES

Dickinson bore the Adams presidency, 1797–1801, without visible reaction, if the eruption over war with France can be left out of the account. The two patriot partners had clashed, but their differences of temperament did not make them actual enemies; those differences rendered them barely acknowledged collaborators in a common enterprise. They rarely if ever spoke directly of each other during Adams's presidency and beyond. (Adams would outlive Dickinson by eighteen years.) At the same time, Dickinson's admiration for Jefferson, who defeated Adams in the landmark election of 1800, flowered as the philosophical division between Republicans and high Federalists intensified. The two men had worked together closely enough for friendship to blossom and for each to understand the other's grounds and intentions. If Adams had little good to say of the Philadelphian who would not adopt his urgency on independence, he had substantially less regard for Jefferson, whose principles stood opposite his own. It was not so much, perhaps, that Adams drove two great men—Jefferson and Dickinson—into each other's arms as that his anger at both helped clarify the terms of their agreement.

Dickinson "was the warm friend of Mr. Jefferson," Stillé writes, "and of his administration, and . . . he was frequently consulted by him in regard to the policy of certain proposed public measures." He had taken a liking to the republican style as embodied by the man he called "My dear friend" in a letter of congratulations on his ascent to the presidency. "As to the past, as far as I am enabled to form a Judgement," Dickinson wrote the new chief executive, "I believe that our Minds have been in perfect Unison." He was viewing in a more accommodating way, it seems, their differences as to the right time for declaring independence. "Perhaps, We are the selected People upon Earth, from whom huge Portions of Mankind are to learn, that Liberty is really a transcendent Blessing, as capable by its enlightened Energies of calmly dissipating its internal Enemies as of triumphantly repelling its foreign Foes." It was his "Ardent Wish" and "fervent Prayer" that God might honor his esteemed friend "as an Instrument for advancing his gracious Purposes, and that he may be thy Guide, and Protector." Jefferson, in response to his "dear & respected Friend," bade "heaven prosper you in your endeavors and long preserve in health & life a consistent patriot, whose principles have stood unchanged by prosperous or adverse time."[24]

Thus the author of the Declaration of Independence to the man whose reputation, as viewed from one angle, rests upon his refusal to sign that very document. It was a peculiar convergence, this latest one, grounded in the deep truths of the revolutionary spirit and program.

"ONE OF THE GREAT WORTHIES OF THE REVOLUTION"

Dickinson would live—improbably enough, given a lifetime of physical miseries and limitations—until February 14, 1808. A fever had laid him low. He sank steadily. Practically the last words he spoke were taken down by one present as "I wish happiness to all mankind, and the blessings of peace to all the nations of the earth, and these are the constant subjects of my prayers."[25]

Five years earlier, Dickinson's wife, Polly—loyal, attentive, the great pillar of his existence—had died, after thirty-three years of marriage. The blow was heavy. As Stillé observes, with accuracy as well as admiration: "No marriage . . . ever proved a truer union. In all the vicissitudes of a life checkered by various fortunes, in triumph or disaster, whether he was suffering under misrepresentations or his acts and motives, or whether he was at last vindicated, honored, and revered, his wife was always his helpmate and best friend." On the occasion of the couple's wedding—outside the very proper environment of the Quaker Meeting—her faintly scandalized uncle wrote of his fear that "she has slipped from the top of the hill of the reputation she had gained in the Society, and that it will be a long time before she gains it again, if ever." Life at "the top of the hill" was an objective for which Mary "Polly" Dickinson displayed no visible craving. She defined her purpose in life as that of lending support to her husband and family in all necessary endeavors—no small matter in the case of a husband whose physical problems compounded his more-than-occasional political difficulties. John, when away from home, as often was the case, proved a diligent correspondent. His "ever dear Polly," as he liked to address her, was the fortunate recipient of affectionate, everyday correspondence spun off by one of the principal literary men of his time and place.[26]

Five Dickinson children were born into the chancy eighteenth-century world of bleedings and purgings meant to relieve common afflictions of which no one, including physicians, knew much. Three of the five died before attaining adulthood; daughters Maria and Sarah (otherwise Sally) survived. Only Maria, who married her second cousin, Albanus Logan, would perpetuate the line. The

Farmer rests in the graveyard of Wilmington's Quaker meeting: the Society of Friends, after all was said and done, having had the last word concerning the earthly John Dickinson.

Jefferson said of him, in a letter to the friend who had informed him of Dickinson's death: "A more estimable man or truer patriot could not have left us.... His name will be consecrated in history as one of the great worthies of the Revolution."[27]

Dickinson's last years had been filled with books and good works, his role in the founding of Dickinson College, near Carlisle, Pennsylvania, prominent among them. The eminent Dr. Benjamin Rush chartered the college in 1783, during Dickinson's presidency of Pennsylvania. Dickinson had underwritten the institution with a conspicuous gift of two plantations and 1,500 books retrieved from Fair Hill after the British put it to the torch. He served until his death as president of the college's board of trustees. Prior to the bestowal of the family name, the institution, a former grammar school, was briefly, touchingly, fittingly in view of the Dickinsons' partnership in all things, called John and Mary's College. Dickinson and Rush contrived the college's official seal: a liberty cap, a telescope, and an open Bible. Liberty, learning, and religion—Dickinson College aimed high. John Dickinson was adamant concerning the role of religion in the schooling and refinement of the mind. He supported a free Quaker-run boarding school in Philadelphia, reasoning that "it is the indispensable duty of those who revere religion to cultivate learning in order to counteract the mischief flowing from its perversions and apply it to its proper use."

To religion he devoted more and more of his study, his pen flowing almost ceaselessly in celebration of Christian truth and understanding. Here was no rationalist-Deist Founder of the sort to which many modern writers point in rebuffing the notion of a new nation dedicated to God, modeling its institutions on His purposes. He spoke of the Bible as the book that "has done more good than all the books in the world; would do much more, if duly regarded; and might lead the objectors against it to happiness, if they would value it as they should."[28]

With the Quakers, the son of an aggrieved Samuel Dickinson achieved something like reconciliation. He used the "plain language" of "thee" and "thou" in his letters and constantly dwelt on the theme of peace—such peace as he had pursued with formidable consistency in the 1760s and the '70s.[29]

The necessity the Revolution had imposed upon lovers of liberty to talk endlessly of liberty had perhaps the unexpected effect of opening eyes and minds to comparable claims that others might assert.[30] Was liberty just for Englishmen? Clearly not. Was it for Americans as well? Certainly—but then, which Americans? Some? All? If for only some, why? On what grounds? Those who claimed the blessings of liberty would increasingly see themselves bound to spread those blessings without differentiation. The language of John Dickinson had its infectious features—not least as it informed the spirit of John Dickinson himself.

LEGACY

The Founding Fathers, it must be plain by this stage in our history, were a highly assorted lot: if not the demigods of legend, then people of remarkable gifts and concentrative powers allocated by nature across a broad range of qualities and defects. It would be a little silly to think of them as drawing collective lightning from the skies, like Franklin with his famous key. Rather, they worked out their collective notions of what to do and how to do it based on earnest discussion of ideas and strategies, at which no founder was more earnest or informed than John Dickinson of Pennsylvania. That he sometimes prevailed, sometimes failed is scarcely the point. He informed; he challenged; he angered; he roused.

History's oddities, we all understand, include the assignment of definitive instances and characteristics to its greater participants—Franklin's rakishness, Jefferson's polymathy, Washington's steadfastness. To this catalog, convention has appended Dickinson's deliberate absence from the Pennsylvania State House on July 2, 1776. A day, by this reckoning, can define a life. The life of John Dickinson has a breadth and depth unsubmissive to such corner cutting, for all the temptations to which the corner cutters, especially those of the entertainment industry, regularly give way. No patriot of Dickinson's day was more intensely patriotic, no lover of liberty more ardent. "Liberty," wrote he, "is the sun of society. Rights are the beams."[31] No expositor of the ideas of liberty wrote with greater learning and eloquence—or enjoyed for a long time more commensurate respect, even veneration.

Side by side with history's oddities are its tricks: matters of timing, matters of appearance and circumstance, great outcomes perfected on account of nearness to the occasion or frustrated for want of a nail. Dickinson's legacy is larger by far than can be conjured from sequenced flashes of lightning. His persistence in seeking essential guarantees for the pursuit of liberty is the legacy to which history will one day pay overdue tribute.

The gift of John Dickinson to succeeding generations is the example of faith in God's authority over human affairs, and in liberty itself as evidence of the human destiny to lives of joy, dignity, and solemn gratitude.

NOTES

INTRODUCTION: "THE MOST UNDERRATED OF ALL THE FOUNDERS"

1   Carl Bridenbaugh, *The Spirit of '76* (New York: Oxford University Press, 1975), 153.

2   Forrest McDonald and Ellen Shapiro McDonald, *Requiem: Variations on Eighteenth-Century Themes* (Lawrence: University Press of Kansas, 1988), 86.

3   Max Farrand, *The Records of the Federal Convention of 1787* (New Haven, CT: Yale University Press, 1911), 3:278.

4   Moses Coit Tyler, *The Literary History of the American Revolution* (New York: Frederick Unger Publishing Co., 1957), 2:28.

5   Jack Rakove, *Revolutionaries: A New History of the Invention of America* (New York: Houghton Mifflin Harcourt, 2010).

6   David McCullough, *John Adams* (New York: Simon and Schuster, 2001), 126.

ONE: "THE FIELDS ARE FULL OF PROMISES"

1   The fullest, most engaging account of the Dickinsons' early North American career can be found in "The House on Jones Neck," an uncopyrighted pamphlet by the Dickinson scholar J. H. Powell, available online at www.historyhome.co.uk/c-eight/America/dick2. htm—a site dedicated to English history and kept efficiently by Dr. Marjie Bloy. I commend both pamphlet and website. See also Charles J. Stillé, *The Life and Times of John Dickinson* (Philadelphia: The Historical Society of Pennsylvania, 1891); Milton E. Flower, *John Dickinson: Conservative Revolutionary* (Charlottesville: University of Virginia Press, 1983); and John A. Munroe, *Colonial Delaware: A History* (Millwood, NY: KTO Press, 1978). Dickinson, born on November 2, according to the Julian calendar then in use in the English-speaking world, added to his birth date the eleven extra days necessitated by adoption of the Gregorian calendar. As did, of course, George Washington—born the same year as Dickinson on the Julian-style date of February 11.

2   Powell, "The House on Jones Neck"; Flower, *John Dickinson*.

3   Isaac Sharpless, *A Quaker Experiment in Government: History of Quaker Government in Pennsylvania, 1682–1783* (Philadelphia: Ferris & Leach, 1902), 95.

4   Stillé, *The Life and Times of John Dickinson*, 307.

5   Daniel Boorstin, *The Americans: The Colonial Experience* (New York: Random House, 1958), 203.

6   Sir William Blackstone, *Commentaries on the Laws of England*, 1:12.

7   Catherine Drinker Bowen, *The Lion and the Throne: The Life and Times of Sir Edward Coke* (Boston: Little Brown, 1957), 305.

8   Sir William Holdsworth, *A History of English Law* (London: Sweet and Maxwell, 1991), 12:78.

9   Ibid., 6:443; Blackstone, *Commentaries on the Laws of England*, 23.

10 Liza Picard, *Dr. Johnson's London* (New York: St. Martin's Griffin, 2002), 203.

11 Boorstin, *The Americans*, 198.

12 H. Trevor Colbourn and Richard Peters, "A Pennsylvania Farmer at the Court of King George: John Dickinson's London Letters, 1754–1756,"

Pennsylvania Magazine of History and Biography 86, no. 3 (July 1962): 249.

13   James Boswell, *The Life of Samuel Johnson* (New York: Heritage Press, 1963), 2:403.

14   Picard, *Dr. Johnson's London*, 3.

15   Colbourn and Peters, "A Pennsylvania Farmer at the Court of King George," 269, 278, 280.

16   Ibid., 280, 267.

17   Ibid., 257, 278, 280.

18   Ibid., 248.

TWO: "AN IMMENSE BUSTLE IN THE WORLD"

1   David Hawke, *In the Midst of a Revolution* (Philadelphia: University of Pennsylvania Press, 1961), 38, 41.

2   W. E. H. Lecky, *The American Revolution, 1763–1783* (New York: D. Appleton and Co., 1913), 20.

3   Stephen S. Lucas, *Portents of Rebellion: Rhetoric and Revolution in Philadelphia, 1765–76* (Philadelphia: Temple University Press, 1976), 15.

4   Kenneth Rossman, *Thomas Mifflin and the Politics of the American Revolution* (Chapel Hill: University of North Carolina Press, 1952), 10–11; Theodore Thayer, *Pennsylvania Politics and the Growth of Democracy, 1740–1776* (Harrisburg: Pennsylvania Historical and Museum Commission, 1953), 69, 79, 97, 107; "Poetical Description of Philadelphia in 1730," *Historical Magazine*, IV (1860): 344; E. Digby Baltzell, *Philadelphia Gentlemen: The Making of a National Upper Class* (New York: Free Press, 1958), 63. Baltzell and also Nathaniel Burt (*The Perennial Philadelphians: The Anatomy of an American Aristocracy* [Boston: Little Brown, 1963]) found the aristocratic ideal more or less alive in Philadelphia on the very eve of the social/cultural cataclysms of the 1960s. So did, for entertainment purposes, the Paul Newman motion picture *The Young Philadelphians* (1959).

5   Hawke, *In the Midst of a Revolution*, 15; John Jordan, "A Description of the State-House, Philadelphia in 1774," *Pennsylvania Magazine of History and Biography* 23, no. 4 (1899): 417.

6   Lucas, *Portents of Rebellion*, 13.

7   Colbourn and Peters, "A Pennsylvania Farmer at the Court of King George," 245.

8   Lyman H. Butterfield et al., eds, *Diary and Autobiography of John Adams* (Cambridge: Belknap Press of Harvard University Press, 1961), 2:117.

9   Colbourn and Peters, "A Pennsylvania Farmer at the Court of King George," 257.

10 Thayer, *Pennsylvania Politics and the Growth of Democracy*, 100; Sharpless, *A Quaker Experiment in Government*, 95–96.

11 Jane E. Calvert, in *Quaker Constitutionalism and the Political Thought of John Dickinson* (New York: Cambridge University Press, 2009), argues that Quaker theory and theology informed Dickinson's conscience respecting questions of government authority. "There is . . . no claim," she writes, "that Dickinson was animated by only Quaker theory; rather, his thought is representative of the ecumenism possible in political Quakerism"—which is "neither Whig nor Tory, liberal nor republican; it is a bit of all with something other." Without disputing the immense value of Dr. Calvert's research, I find it fruitful, given the historical record, to speak of Dickinson's convictions as framed essentially by his historical knowledge, legal learning, and personal love of liberty.

12 Stillé, *The Life and Times of John Dickinson*, 308.

13 Benjamin Kite, "Recollections of Philadelphia Near Seventy Years Ago," *Pennsylvania Magazine of History and Biography*, 19 (1895): 2; American Periodicals Series Online, 264.

14 Stillé, *The Life and Times of John Dickinson*, 37.

15 In a recent scholarly ranking of neglected Founders, Wilson received the most points by a significant margin. See Gary L. Gregg II and Mark David Hall, *America's Forgotten Founders*, second edition (Wilmington, DE: ISI Books, 2012), xv.

16 Stillé, *The Life and Times of John Dickinson*, 38.

17 Thayer, *Pennsylvania Politics and the Growth of Democracy*, 5; Winfred Trexler Root, *The Relations of Pennsylvania with the British Government, 1696–1765* (New York: AMS Press, 1969), 5, 40; Stillé, *The Life and Times of John Dickinson*, 42.

18 H. W. Brands, *The First American: The Life and Times of Benjamin*

Franklin (New York: Doubleday, 2000), 356; David L. Jacobson, "John Dickinson's Fight against Royal Government, 1764," *William and Mary Quarterly*, 3rd series, vol. 19, no. 1 (January 1962): 68.

19 J. H. Hutson, *Pennsylvania Politics, 1746–1770: The Movement for Royal Government and Its Consequences* (Princeton, NJ: Princeton University, 1972), 162.

20 Paul Leicester Ford, ed., *The Writings of John Dickinson*, vol. 1, *Political Writings, 1764–1774* (Philadelphia: Historical Society of Pennsylvania, 1895), 22ff.

21 Benjamin Newcomb, *Franklin and Galloway: A Political Partnership* (New Haven, CT: Yale University Press, 1972), 89–90.

22 Edmund Burke, *Reflections on the Revolution in France* (New Rochelle, NY: Arlington House, undated), 45, 74; M. E. Bradford, *A Worthy Company: Brief Lives of the Framers of the Constitution* (Marlborough, NH: Plymouth Rock Foundation, 1982), 107.

23 Hutson, *Pennsylvania Politics*, 247.

24 Ford, *The Writings of John Dickinson*, 48.

THREE: "YOU RIVET PERPETUAL CHAINS UPON YOUR UNHAPPY COUNTRY"

1 McCullough, *John Adams*, 89.

2 Ford, *The Writings of John Dickinson*, 267.

3 Gordon Wood, *The American Revolution: A History* (New York: Modern Library, 2002), 7.

4 Edmund S. and Helen M. Morgan, *The Stamp Act Crisis: Prologue to Revolution* (Chapel Hill: University of North Carolina, 1953), 84; Randolph Greenfield Adams, *Political Ideas of the American Revolution* (New York: Facsimile Library, 1939), 78.

5 Ford, *The Writings of John Dickinson*, 184.

6 Ibid., 183–87.

7 Ibid., 193–96.

8 Ibid., 199–205.

9 Ibid., 262–63.

10 Ibid., 234–43.

11 O. A. Sherrard, *Lord Chatham and America* (London: The Bodley Head, 1958), 185–86.

12 Ross J. S. Hoffman and Paul Levack, eds., *Burke's Politics* (New York: Knopf, 1949), 51.

13 Sherrard, *Lord Chatham and America*, 186.

14 Hoffman and Levack, *Burke's Politics*, 52–53.

FOUR: "MY DEAR COUNTRYMEN"

1 John Dickinson, *Letters from a Farmer in Pennsylvania*, in Forrest McDonald, ed., *Empire and Nation: Letters from a Farmer in Pennsylvania (John Dickinson) and Letters from the Federal Farmer (Richard Henry Lee)*, second edition (Indianapolis: Liberty Fund, 1999), 3.

2 Ibid., 17.

3 Ibid., 17.

4 Ibid., 6.

5 Ibid., 4, 6.

6 Ibid., 10–11, 14.

7 Ibid., 19–20; Robert Middlekauff, *The Glorious Cause: The American Revolution, 1763–1789* (Oxford/New York: Oxford University Press, 2005), 162.

8 Dickinson, *Letters from a Farmer in Pennsylvania*, 21–33.

9 Ibid., 43–44.

10 Ibid., 44.; J. C. Long, *Mr. Pitt and America's Birthright* (London: Frederick A. Stokes Company, 1940), 439.

11 Dickinson, *Letters from a Farmer in Pennsylvania*, 73, 58, 60, 75, 77.

12 Ibid., 79–81.

13 Ibid., 84.

14 McDonald, *Empire and Nation*, xiii; Philip Davidson, *Propaganda and the American Revolution, 1768–1783* (Chapel Hill: University of North Carolina Press, 1941), 243; Jacobson, "John Dickinson's Fight against Royal Government," 55–56; Pauline Maier, *From Resistance to Revolution: Colonial Radicals and the Development of American Opposition to Britain, 1765–1776* (New York: Knopf, 1972); Tyler, *The Literary History of the American Revolution*, 1:234–38.

15   Leonard W. Labaree, ed., *The Papers of Benjamin Franklin* (New Haven, CT: Yale University Press, 1970), 15:75, 111; Tyler, *The Literary History of the American Revolution*, 1:234–38.

16   Ibid., 75.

FIVE: "IN FREEDOM WE'RE BORN, AND IN FREEDOM WE'LL LIVE"

1   The Norris fortune alone is reckoned at between 50,000 and 80,000 pounds, a sum worth indeterminable millions in twenty-first-century terms. J. C. Furnas, *The Americans: A Social History of the United States, 1587–1914* (New York: Putnam's, 1969), 197.

2   Thomas Wendel, "The Speaker of the House, Pennsylvania, 1701–1776," *Pennsylvania Magazine of History and Biography* 97, no. 1 (January 1973): 15.

3   Stillé, *The Life and Times of John Dickinson*, 311–12.

4   Ibid., 317.

5   Tyler, *The Literary History of the American Revolution*, 2:27; *Songs and Ballads of the American Revolution* (New York: D. Appleton & Co., 1856), 36.

6   *Songs and Ballads*, 36–37.

7   Davidson, *Propaganda and the American Revolution*, 189.

8   Jacobson, "John Dickinson's Fight against Royal Government," 68.

9   Claude H. Van Tyne, *England and America: Rivals in the American Revolution* (New York: Russell and Russell, 1927), 104.

SIX: "THERE IS A SPIRIT OF LIBERTY AMONG US"

1   Ford, *The Writings of John Dickinson*, 451–52.

2   Ibid., 455–62.

3   Ibid.

4   Hoffman and Levack, *Burke's Politics*, 56–61. Among Burke's asseverations: "Again, and again, revert to your old principles—seek peace and ensure it—leave America, if she has taxable matter in her, to tax herself."

5   Frank Gaylord Cook, "John Dickinson," *Atlantic Monthly*, 65 (January 1890): 77.

6   Bradford, *A Worthy Company*, 107.

7   Hoffman and Levack, *Burke's Politics*, 58.

8   Stillé, *The Life and Times of John Dickinson*, 106.

9   Boyd Stanley Schlenther, *Charles Thomson: A Patriot's Pursuit* (Newark: University of Delaware Press, 1990), 104.

10   Stillé, *The Life and Times of John Dickinson*, 107–8.

SEVEN: "THE FORCE OF ACCUMULATED INJURIES"

1   Butterfield, *Diary and Autobiography of John Adams*, 2:117.

2   Ibid., 133, 135, 147.

3   For all their subsequent differences, as to viewpoint and action Adams and Dickinson reasoned from essentially the same premises. Both were good lawyers. Both claimed the chartered rights of Englishmen, to borrow Burke's famous phrase. In his *Dissertation on the Common and Feudal Law*, Adams found Americans "under an historical obligation to protect invasion of their rights and to resist any resurrection of canon and feudal tyranny." See H. Trevor Colbourn, *The Lamp of Experience: Whig History and the Intellectual Origins of the American Revolution* (Chapel Hill: University of North Carolina Press, 1965), 87–90. For Adams's impatience with opposition, see Joseph Ellis, *Passionate Sage: The Character and Legacy of John Adams* (New York: Norton, 1983), 44–46.

4   Edmund Cody Burnett, *The Continental Congress* (New York: Macmillan, 1941), 43; Stillé, *The Life and Times of John Dickinson*, 138–39.

5   Ernest H. Baldwin, "Joseph Galloway, The Loyalist Politician: a Supporter of Law and Order. Speaker of Assembly. A Delegate to Congress," *Pennsylvania Magazine of History and Biography* 26, no. 3 (1902): 289.

6   Samuel Eliot Morison, *Sources and Documents Illustrating the American Revolution 1764–1788* (Oxford: Clarendon Press, 1929), 116–18.

7   Ibid., 188–22.

8   Ibid., 122–25.

9   Stillé, *The Life and Times of John Dickinson*, 142–43.

10   From the Address of Congress to the Inhabitants of Quebec: "All [the histories of various nations] demonstrate the truth of this simple position, that to live by the will of one man, or set of men, is the production of misery to all men. On the solid foundation of this principle, *Englishmen* reared up the fabric of their constitution with such a strength, as for ages to defy time, tyranny, treachery, internal and foreign wars.... The first grand right is that of the people having a share in their own government by their representatives chose [*sic*] by themselves, and in consequence of being ruled by laws, which they themselves approve, not by edicts of men over whom they have no controul. This is a bulwark surrounding and defending their property, which by their honest cares and labours they have acquired, so that no portion of it can legally be taken from them, but with their own full and free consent, when they in their judgment deem it just and necessary to give them for public services, and precisely direct the easiest, cheapest, and most equal methods in which they shall be collected." *The Political Writings of John Dickinson, Esquire* (Wilmington, DE: Bonsal and Niles, 1801), 2:3–18.

11   Edmund C. Burnett, *Letters of Members of the Continental Congress* (August 29, 1774, to July 4, 1776), 6:83.

12   Butterfield, *Diary and Autobiography of John Adams*, 157.

EIGHT: "TO DIE FREE-MEN RATHER THAN TO LIVE LIKE SLAVES"

1   Sharpless, *A Quaker Experiment in Government*, 76; Stillé, *The Life and Times of John Dickinson*, 124–25.

2   McCullough, *John Adams*, 94.

3   Jacobson, "John Dickinson's Fight against Royal Government," 2.

4   Rakove, *Revolutionaries*, 82.

5   Hoffman and Levack, *Burke's Politics*, 69, 68, 77, 94.

6   Jacobson, "John Dickinson's Fight against Royal Government," 83.

7   Louis W. Potts, *Arthur Lee: A Virtuous Revolutionary* (Baton Rouge: Louisiana State University Press, 1981), 139.

8   Jacobson, "John Dickinson's Fight against Royal Government," 89.

9   *The Political Writings of John Dickinson, Esquire*, 2:45–52.

10   Pauline Maier, *American Scripture: Making the Declaration of Independence* (New York: Knopf, 1997), 20.

11   Morison, *Sources and Documents Illustrating the American Revolution*, 141–45.

12   Ibid.

13   Burnett, *Letters of Members of the Continental Congress* 1:88.

14   Burnett, *The Continental Congress*, 87.

15   Burnett, *Letters of Members of the Continental Congress*, 1:108–9.

16   Ibid., 176.

17   Butterfield, *Diary and Autobiography of John Adams*, 2:173.

NINE: "WAR IS ACTUALLY BEGUN"

1   Burnett, *Letters of Members of the Continental Congress*, 1:157.

2   B. D. Bargar, *Lord Dartmouth and the American Revolution* (Columbia: University of South Carolina Press, 1965), 156–59.

3   McCullough, *John Adams*, 18.

4   Burnett, *Letters of Members of the Continental Congress*, 1:173.

5   Lucas, *Portents of Rebellion*, 155.

6   Ibid., 157.

7   Charles A. Beard, *An Economic Interpretation of the Constitution of the United States* (New York: Macmillan, 1913).

8   Calvert, *Quaker Constitutionalism and the Political Thought of John Dickinson*, 233.

9   Burnett, *Letters of Members of the Continental Congress*, 1:349.

10   *Common Sense* has over the centuries gone through numberless editions. Employed in the present work is *Basic Writings of Thomas Paine: Common Sense, Rights of Man, Age of Reason* (New York: Willey, 1942). For Adams's sentiments, see Maier, *American Scripture*, 31.

11   Merrill Jensen, ed., *Tracts of the American Revolution: 1763–1776* (Indianapolis: Bobbs-Merrill, 1967), 448–49.

TEN: "LET MY COUNTRY TREAT ME AS SHE PLEASES"

1   Jacobson, "John Dickinson's Fight against Royal Government," 107.

2   Stillé, *The Life and Times of John Dickinson*, 165.

3   Burnett, *Letters of Members of the Continental Congress*, 1:461.

4   Ibid., 188.

5   Hawke, *In the Midst of a Revolution*, 166.

6   Julian P. Boyd, ed., *The Papers of Thomas Jefferson* (Princeton, NJ: Princeton University Press, 1960), 1:309.

7   Burnett, *Letters of Members of the Continental Congress*, 1:476–77.

8   Boyd, *The Papers of Thomas Jefferson*, 1:311.

9   Maier, *American Scripture*, 66; Jacobson, "John Dickinson's Fight against Royal Government," 111–12.

10 Peter Stone and Sherman Edwards, *1776: A Musical Play* (New York: Viking, 1964), 90–92.

11 Stillé, *The Life and Times of John Dickinson*, 192.

12 Jacobson, "John Dickinson's Fight against Royal Government," 112–13.

13 Stillé, *The Life and Times of John Dickinson*, 190–92.

ELEVEN: "THE FINISHING BLOW"

1   John H. Powell, "Speech of John Dickinson Opposing the Declaration of Independence," *Pennsylvania Magazine of History and Biography* 65 (October 1941): 458–81. For the rendering of Dickinson's crabbed, barely legible handwriting into readable form, Powell is due vast credit.

2   Butterfield, *Diary and Autobiography of John Adams*, 3:396.

3   Ibid., 396–97.

4   Morris afterward duly signed the Declaration. James Wilson, an opponent until virtually the end, voted for adoption and signed.

5   Forrest McDonald and Ellen Shapiro McDonald, *Requiem: Variations on Eighteenth-Century Themes* (Lawrence: University Press of Kansas, 1988), 89.

6   M. E. Bradford, *A Better Guide Than Reason: Studies in the American Revolution* (La Salle, IL: Sherwood Sugden & Co., 1979), 96.

7   Schlenther, *Charles Thomson*, 139.

8   Calvert, *Quaker Constitutionalism and the Political Thought of John Dickinson*, 245, 243.

9   Ibid., 242.

10 Schlenther, *Charles Thomson*, 139.

11 Ibid., 139–40.

12 There was in Galloway's story a large component of tragedy. Like Dickinson, he had ambition, large land holdings, and significant gifts as a lawyer. Unlike Dickinson, he possessed more than a touch of arrogance and impatience. He "apparently had no sense of humor at all," according to Benjamin Newcomb. "He took himself and the world very seriously.... He acted as if he did not need to flatter or conciliate others." Even friends found him overbearing. He never could see why his fellow Americans could not see as clearly as he could the bounteous advantages of life under British authority. Like so many other American loyalists, he paid a heavy price for his choice of allegiances. A lynch mob threatened him on one occasion; a Philadelphia newspaper denounced him as "a traitor to his country and its laws." The British, during their occupation of Philadelphia, made him the city's civil governor. Then they evacuated. There was nothing for it, on Galloway's part, but to cross the ocean and live in England, never to return. He died August 29, 1803, at Watford, Herts. The government in which he had reposed such trust granted him and his family a pension of 500 pounds a year. His estate, at the time of its confiscation by Pennsylvania, had been worth approximately 40,000 pounds. See Ernest H. Baldwin, "Joseph Galloway, The Loyalist Politician: A Youth and Lawyer. A Member of Assembly. An Opponent of Proprietors," *Pennsylvania Magazine of History and Biography* 26, no. 2 (1902): 161; Ernest H. Baldwin, "Joseph Galloway, Author of Plan of Union. Tory Suspect. Tory. Conclusion," *Pennsylvania Magazine of History and Biography* 26, no. 4 (1902): 47; and Benjamin H. Newcomb, *Franklin and Galloway: A Political Partnership* (New Haven, CT: Yale University Press, 1972), 9–10.

13 Calvert, *Quaker Constitutionalism and the Political Thought of John Dickinson*, 245.

TWELVE: "WILLINGLY TO RESIGN MY LIFE"

1   Stillé, *The Life and Times of John Dickinson*, 204.

2   Ibid., 202–3.

3   Burnett, *Letters of Members of the Continental Congress*, 4:451.

4   R. R. Logan Collection of John Dickinson Papers, Historical Society of Pennsylvania; *The Papers of Benjamin Franklin*, 22:5; Jacobson, "John Dickinson's Fight against Royal Government," 119; Stillé, *The Life and Times of John Dickinson*, 202.

5   John Adams served the military enterprise at a technically higher level as chairman of the Board of War and Ordnance before becoming commissioner to France.

6   Stillé, *The Life and Times of John Dickinson*, 202–3.

7   Garry Wills, *Inventing America: Jefferson's Declaration of Independence* (New York: Doubleday, 1978), 232.

8   Merrill Jensen, *The Articles of Confederation* (Madison: University of Wisconsin Press, 1948), 126.

9   Jack Rakove, *The Beginnings of National Politics: An Interpretative History of the Continental Congress* (New York: Knopf, 1979), 152.

10 The received, as it were, Dickinson draft of the Articles is found in Jensen, *The Articles of Confederation*, 254–62. I am indebted to five Hillsdale College students of Professor John P. Willson—Amy Anderson, Merrie Kreuger, Kyle Payne, Sarah Streck, and Alex Swem—for transcribing from Dickinson's crabbed handwriting an earlier version containing a grant in broad terms of religious freedom "without the least abridgement" of civil rights. The passage was dropped in committee.

11 Jensen, *The Articles of Confederation*, 127.

12 Rakove, *The Beginnings of National Politics*, 152.

13 Jensen, *The Articles of Confederation*, 258–61.

14 Burnett, *Letters of Members of the Continental Congress*, 1:517.

15 Jensen, *The Articles of Confederation*, 130.

16 Ibid., 175.

17 McDonald and McDonald, *Requiem*, 19.

18 Ibid., 89–90.

19 Stillé, *The Life and Times of John Dickinson*, 206.

20 Forrest McDonald, *E Pluribus Unum: The Formation of the American Republic, 1776–1790* (Boston: Houghton Mifflin, 1965), 37.

21 Stillé, *The Life and Times of John Dickinson*, 217.

22 J. H. Powell, "John Dickinson and the Constitution," *Pennsylvania Magazine of History and Biography* 60, no. 1 (January 1936).

23 Stillé, *The Life and Times of John Dickinson*, 394.

24 John W. Jordan, "Sessions of the Continental Congress Held in the College of Philadelphia in July, 1778," *Pennsylvania Magazine of History and Biography* 27, no. 1 (1898): 114.

25 Tyler, *The Literary History of the American Revolution*, 2:4.

THIRTEEN: "THE SACRED VOICE OF MY COUNTRY"

1 Burnett, *Letters of Members of the Continental Congress*, 4:257.

2 John A. Munroe, *Colonial Delaware: A History* (Millwood, NY: KTO Press, 1978), 254.

3 J. H. Powell, "John Dickinson as President of Pennsylvania," *Pennsylvania Magazine of History and Biography* 28, no. 3 (July 1961): 258.

4 Stillé, *The Life and Times of John Dickinson*, 227.

5 Robert L. Brunhouse, *The Counter-Revolution in Pennsylvania* (New York: Octagon Books, 1971), 121.

6 Stillé, *The Life and Times of John Dickinson*, 266.

7 Brunhouse, *The Counter-Revolution in Pennsylvania*, 123; Stillé, *The Life and Times of John Dickinson*, 423.

8 Stillé, *The Life and Times of John Dickinson*, 238.

9 Ibid., 364–414. All following quotations are from this text.

10 Ibid., 385.

11 Ibid., 409.

FOURTEEN: "ACTING BEFORE THE WORLD"

1 Charles Warren, *The Making of the Constitution* (Boston: Little, Brown, 1928), 17–18.

2 Max Farrand, *The Records of the Federal Convention of 1787*, 3:6. Dick-

inson's fellow Delaware delegates were George Read (his longtime friend), Gunning Bedford Jr., Richard Barsett, and Jacob Brown. Farrand, *The Records of the Federal Convention of 1787*, 3:558.

3   James Madison, *Journal of the Federal Convention*, ed. E. H. Scott, (Chicago: Albert, Scott & Co., 1893), 96.

4   Ibid., 58.

5   Farrand, *The Records of the Federal Convention of 1787*, 4:67; Stillé, *The Life and Times of John Dickinson*, 258; "Notes of Major William Pierce on the Federal Convention of 1787," *American Historical Review* 3 (January 1898): 329.

6   Catherine Drinker Bowen, *Miracle at Philadelphia* (Boston: Atlantic/ Little Brown, 1966), 103.

7   John Dickinson, *The Letters of Fabius in 1788 on the Federal Constitution* (Whitefish, MT: Kessinger Publishing, 2004), 51.

8   James H. Hutson, "John Dickinson at the Federal Constitutional Convention," *William and Mary Quarterly*, 3rd series, vol. 40, no. 2 (April 1983): 263, 270.

9   Farrand, *The Records of the Federal Convention of 1787*, 1:86.

10   Forrest McDonald, *Novus Ordo Seclorum: The Intellectual Origins of the Constitution* (Lawrence: University Press of Kansas, 1985), 215.

11   Farrand, *The Records of the Federal Convention of 1787*, 1:86–87.

12   Ibid., 158–59.

13   McDonald, *Novus Ordo Seclorum*, 179, 182.

14   Farrand, *The Records of the Federal Convention of 1787*, 1:156–57.

15   Ibid., 156.

16   Hutson, "John Dickinson at the Federal Constitutional Convention," 267; Farrand, *The Records of the Federal Convention of 1787*, 2:207.

17   Hutson, "John Dickinson at the Federal Constitutional Convention," 279–80.

18   Ibid., 276.

19   Stillé, *The Life and Times of John Dickinson*, 329–30; Jane E. Calvert, notes on "Manumission of John Dickinson's Slaves, May 12, 1777– March 27, 1779," R. R. Logan Collection of John Dickinson Papers, Historical Society of Pennsylvania, digitalhistory.hsp.org/node/7549; Frederick B. Tolles, *George Logan of Philadelphia* (New York: Oxford University Press, 1953), 262.

20 Hutson, "John Dickinson at the Federal Constitutional Convention," 280.

21 James H. Hutson, ed., *Supplement to Max Farrand's "The Records of the Federal Convention of 1787"* (New Haven, CT: Yale University Press, 1987), 158.

22 Ibid., 274.

23 Hutson, "John Dickinson at the Federal Constitutional Convention," 272.

FIFTEEN: "EXPERIENCE MUST BE OUR ONLY GUIDE"

1 Dickinson, *The Letters of Fabius*, 2.

2 Publius, *The Federalist Papers* (New Rochelle, NY: Arlington House, 1966), 36.

3 Farrand, *The Records of the Federal Convention of 1787*, 1:278. Jane Calvert (*Quaker Constitutionalism and the Political Thought of John Dickinson*, 285) sees "experience" as meaning, to Dickinson, something larger than common-law customs—namely, divine revelation "or the experience of God in one's conscience." Note Dickinson's testimony (*The Letters of Fabius*, 27) concerning the usefulness of "a knowledge of the distinguishing features of nations . . . their manners, customs, and institutions, the sources of events, their progresses, and determining causes.... Thus one nation may become prudent and happy, not only by the wisdom and success, but even by the errors and misfortunes of another."

4 Dickinson, *The Letters of Fabius*, 20.

5 Ibid., 30–31.

6 Ibid., 53.

7 Ibid., 17, 42.

8 Ibid., 14. The biblical citation is Micah 4:4—a description of the delights in store for the Lord's people once swords have been duly beaten into plowshares.

9 Ibid., 46.

10 Ibid., 11, 12

11 Stillé, *The Life and Times of John Dickinson*, 274.

12 Gregory Ahern, "The Spirit of American Constitutionalism: John Dickinson's *Fabius Letters*," *Humanitas* 11, no. 2 (1998), www.nhinet. org/ahern.htm.

13 Ibid.

14 Dickinson, *The Letters of Fabius*, 18.

15 Stillé, *The Life and Times of John Dickinson*, 278–79.

16 Ibid., 277.

17 Ibid., 280.

18 Saul K. Padover, ed., *Thomas Jefferson on Democracy* (New York: New American Library, 1958), 163.

19 John Emerich Edward Dalberg-Acton, *Lectures on the French Revolution* (Indianapolis: Liberty Fund, 2000), 32.

20 Hoffman and Levack, *Burke's Politics*, 440.

21 *The Political Writings of John Dickinson, Esquire* (Whitefish, MT: Kessinger Publishing, 2010), 2:268, 262–64, 269.

22 Ibid., 170–72.

23 Ibid., 240.

24 Stillé, *The Life and Times of John Dickinson*, 277; Boyd, *The Papers of Thomas Jefferson*, 33:31–32; 34:617.

25 Stillé, *The Life and Times of John Dickinson*, 336.

26 Ibid., 319, 317.

27 Ibid., 336.

28 Dickinson, *The Letters of Fabius*, 25.

29 Stillé, *The Life and Times of John Dickinson*, 329–30; Tolles, *George Logan of Philadelphia*, 262.

30 Dickinson, *The Letters of Fabius*, 24.

31 Ibid.

ACKNOWLEDGMENTS

JEREMY BEER, WHILE EDITOR of ISI Books, commissioned this work—the first biography of John Dickinson since Milton Flower's meticulous treatise in 1962. I am grateful for Mr. Beer's confidence in project and author alike. To the present editor, nonetheless, I owe special thanks for acuity and—something harder to manage—tact, employed in labors over the actual manuscript. Jed Donahue raised more than occasional points that had not thitherto occurred to me. This is why writers, who pretend to despise editors, don't mean a word of what they say. Or, if they do mean it, they belong in a padded cell.

Three scholars were kind enough to run their respective "jewelers' eyes" over every word of the manuscript and make comments from which I profited greatly. Professor Forrest McDonald, one of the most penetrating commentators on the Founding period, is a fellow Texan long resident at the University of Alabama. He was especially generous with his insights, not to mention rapid in supplying them. Professor John Willson, the former Hillsdale College historian, who has a particular affection for John Dickinson, was keen to see that Dickinson's work on the Articles of Confederation received due attention. I hope I have done right by that expectation. Professor George B. Forgie of the University of Texas–Austin shares with me a reverence for the late Professor David M. Potter of Stanford University, under whom we both studied as graduate students. Professor Forgie, a specialist in eighteenth- and nineteeth-century American history, usefully read Dickinson's career against a backdrop innocent of lace cuffs and curlicued signatures. Professor Jack Rakove of Stanford University, eminent for his knowledge of the Dickinson period, courteously made time to speak with and advise me while I was resident at Stanford as a Hoover Institution media fellow.

To Nancy Taylor Murchison, university valedictorian, discerning critic, wife of four decades, I offer special thanks. She accommodated with good cheer and significant encouragement my absences at the library, the office, and out-of-town venues where I sought enlightenment concerning a man too little appreciated, too little understood, for the brains and courage she herself came to appreciate in full measure. She has my continued gratitude for... everything.

INDEX

Achaean League, 201
Adams, Abigail, 92
Adams, John: the "Boston
    Massacre" and, 77; breach
    with Dickinson, 112, 114–17;
    committee memberships in the
    Second Continental Congress,
    138, 140; defense of the
    Declaration of Independence,
    147–48; on Dickinson as a
    colonel in the Philadelphia
    militia, 124; on Dickinson's
    argumentation against the
    Declaration of Independence,
    147; on Dickinson's mother
    and wife, 105; on Dickinson's
    physical appearance, 25, 91;
    difference in temperament with
    Dickinson, 135; at the First
    Continental Congress, 91–92;
impressions of Dickinson in
    1774, 91–92, 98–99; loyalty
    to Great Britain, 38; modern
    media portrayals of, 1–2, 139,
    148; Olive Branch Petition and,
    111, 112; on Paine and *Common
    Sense*, 126; pressures applied
    to Pennsylvania to accept
    the course of independence,
    127–28, 133–34; relations with
    Dickinson during the Adams
    presidency, 211; relations
    with France as president, 209;
    response to Dickinson's "The
    Liberty Song," 73; on the
    "total neglect and disgrace" of
    Dickinson in 1777, 169; views
    of American sovereignty, 75;
    views of a Quaker influence on
    Dickinson, 104, 105